PROGRESSIVE PIONEER

HISTORY OF SCHOOLS & SCHOOLING

Alan R. Sadovnik and Susan F. Semel
General Editors

Vol. 48

PETER LANG
New York • Washington, D.C./Baltimore • Bern
Frankfurt am Main • Berlin • Brussels • Vienna • Oxford

William G. Wraga

Progressive Pioneer

Alexander James Inglis (1879–1924) and American Secondary Education

PETER LANG
New York • Washington, D.C./Baltimore • Bern
Frankfurt am Main • Berlin • Brussels • Vienna • Oxford

Library of Congress Cataloging-in-Publication Data

Wraga, William G.
Progressive pioneer: Alexander James Inglis (1879–1924)
and American secondary education / William G. Wraga.
p. cm. — (History of schools and schooling: vol. 48)
Includes bibliographical references and index.
1. Education, Secondary—United States—History.
2. Progressive education—United States—History.
3. Inglis, Alexander James, 1879–1924—Biography. I. Title.
LA222.W725 370.92—dc22[B] 2007004410
ISBN 978-1-4331-0047-5 (hardcover)
ISBN 978-0-8204-8116-6 (paperback)
ISSN 1089-0678

Bibliographic information published by **Die Deutsche Bibliothek**.
Die Deutsche Bibliothek lists this publication in the "Deutsche Nationalbibliografie"; detailed bibliographic data is available on the Internet at http://dnb.ddb.de/.

Cover design by Joni Holst
Front cover photo credit: Special Collections, Monroe C. Gutman Library,
Harvard University Graduate School of Education

29 Broadway, 18th floor, New York, NY 10006
www.peterlang.com

To Amy Jeanne

Table of Contents

Illustrations

Acknowledgments

The discrepancy between Daniel Tanner and Laurel Tanner's and Herbert Kliebard's representations of Alexander Inglis's *Principles of Secondary Education* excited my interest sufficiently to inspire me to attempt a systematic reconstruction of Inglis's lifework. My first debt of gratitude is to these curriculum historians for fostering a climate of inquiry and of stimulative contention in the field of curriculum history.

Because Inglis left no organized papers, the work of librarians, archivists, and other people with access to information about him was crucial to this study. The following individuals deserve special thanks: David Ment and Betty Weneck, formerly of Special Collections, Millbank Memorial Library, Teachers College, Columbia University; Brian A. Sullivan and Patrice Donoghue, Harvard University Archives; Marylene Altieri and Gladys Dratch, Gutman Library, Harvard University Graduate School of Education; Virginia Feher, University of Georgia Interlibrary Loan; Ida Gegg, Ithaca, NY; Anita Wright, Cortland County, NY, Historical Society; Linda Chiochios, Belmont, CA, Library; Caroline Fisher, Belmont, CA, Historical Society; Grace Wiley, Foreside, ME; David S. McElwain, Houghton Mifflin Company; Elizabeth A. Falsey, The Houghton Library, Harvard University; Thomas Frusciano, Special Collections and University Archives, Rutgers University; Evelyn Lannon, Boston Public Library; Elizabeth Swaim, Special Collections, Wesleyan University; Judy Jessup, Alumni Affairs and Development, The Kiski School, Saltsburg, PA; Kathy Ahern, Russell Library, Middletown, CT; Dione Longley, Middlesex County, CT, Historical Society; and Betty Enos Costa, Town Clerk, Swansea, MA.

I am particularly indebted to David M. Brooks of Bedford, NH, Inglis's nephew, for permission to access Inglis's confidential records, for providing Inglis's few surviving effects for use in this study, and for his hospitality during my visit to his home in February 1997.

This study benefited from feedback on papers presented at the annual meetings of the Society for the Study of Curriculum History and the History of Education Society. Previously published portions of this study benefited from the critical comments of anonymous reviewers and from the constructive guidance of sympathetic editors. Ronald Cervero of the University of Georgia, Lori Bowen, who is a former student of mine at the University of Georgia, O. L. Davis, Jr of the University of Texas at Austin, Craig Kridel of the University of South Carolina, Wesley Null of Baylor University, and Milton Gaither of Messiah College, each read an early draft and generously offered invaluable suggestions that went a long way toward improving this study. This study benefited indirectly from two historian colleagues of mine at the University of Georgia: Ronald Butchart, who introduced me to prosopography, and Derrick Alridge, with whom I enjoy frequent productive conversations about the history of education. I am especially grateful to Alan Sadovnik and Susan Semel, series editors at Peter Lang Publishing, for their input to and support of my scholarship. Despite the help of my colleagues, I alone assume responsibility for the shortcomings of this work.

During spring 2006, a Faculty Research Leave from the College of Education and the Department of Lifelong Education, Administration, and Policy at the University of Georgia provided blocks of uninterrupted time to prepare this manuscript. Over the past ten years, the University of Georgia Research Foundation, the University of Georgia College of Education, and the Departments of Educational Leadership and of Educational Administration and Policy at the University of Georgia provided financial support to conduct archival research for this study.

Permission to quote from archival material was provided by courtesy of the following institutions: Special Collections and Archives, Wesleyan University Library; the Gottesman Libraries, Teachers College, Columbia University; Special Collections, Gutman Library, Harvard University; the Houghton Library, Harvard University; Harvard University Libraries; University of Colorado at Boulder Libraries; and the Seeley G. Mudd Manuscript Library, Princeton University Libraries.

Parts of the introduction and chapter seven previously appeared as William G. Wraga, "Progressive Pioneer: Alexander James Inglis (1879–1924) and American Secondary Education," *Teachers College Record* 108 (June 2006), 1080–105; part of chapter four previously appeared as William G. Wraga, "A Progressive Legacy Squandered: The *Cardinal Principles* Report Reconsidered," *History of Education Quarterly* 41 (Winter 2001), 494–519; this material is reprinted here with permission of Blackwell Publishing. An earlier version of chapter five previously appeared as William G. Wraga, "The Inglis Surveys: Social Efficiency Thesis Anomalies," in *Explorations in Curriculum History*, ed. Sherry L. Field and Lynn Burlbaw (Greenwich, CT: Information Age, Publishing, Inc., 2005), 13–18; this material is reprinted here in agreement with Information Age Publishing. Part of chapter six previously appeared as William G. Wraga, "The Progressive Classicism of Alexander James Inglis," *The Classical Journal* 99 (October–November 2003), 59–69 and William G. Wraga, "The Posthumous Redaction of a Progressive Classicist," *The Classical Journal* 99 (December–January 2003–4), 169–75; this material is reprinted here with permission of the Classical Association of the Middle West and South.

Introduction

Alexander James Inglis pioneered the systematic study of secondary education in the United States. Inglis's *Principles of Secondary Education*, published in 1918, represented the first comprehensive review, appraisal, and synthesis of research, theory, and practice in secondary education. It presented an exhaustive articulation of the emerging comprehensive high school model. As a "scientific" attempt to generate organizing principles upon which to construct a responsive social institution, *Principles of Secondary Education* stands as a quintessential statement of progressive values. As both a critique and a reconstruction of traditional forms of secondary education, it represents an expression of American pragmatism in education. For decades *Principles* "set the pattern for countless other books in the field" of secondary education.[1] Also, it informed the implementation of the comprehensive high school model in the United States. Yet in the historical literature Inglis's work has remained relatively obscure, overshadowed by contemporaries who lived longer to establish enduring reputations.

Most historians writing about education in the early twentieth-century United States have overlooked Inglis's career, which, in its day, was as high profile as it was brief. In 1924 Inglis died unexpectedly at the age of forty-four. Historians who have not overlooked him have depicted Inglis's work in contradictory ways. Kliebard, for example, regarded Inglis's book *Principles of Secondary Education* as a work of individual genius that transcended contemporary educational and social trends and distanced Inglis's ideas from the *Cardinal Principles* report.[2] Powell, in his history of the Harvard University Graduate School of Education, considered Inglis's work largely an unoriginal reflection of the new social approach to secondary education that paralleled the *Cardinal Principles* report. Tanner and Tanner depicted Inglis as a key contributor to the *Cardinal Principles* report and as a farsighted architect of the comprehensive high school ideal.[3] These conflicting assessments are based almost exclusively on reference to Inglis's 1918 treatise, *Principles of Secondary Education*, an appropriate focus, since *Principles* clearly stands as Inglis's magnum opus. Widely used in its day, for decades after its publication, Inglis's book was a standard citation in secondary education textbooks. Most significantly, perhaps, J. B. Conant's thinking about the comprehensive high school owed a great, explicit debt to Inglis.

Yet *Principles* represented just one of Inglis's remarkable accomplishments. He began his career as a Latin teacher, coauthored three Latin textbooks and, as befit an aspiring classicist, translated Cicero's *Essay on Friendship*. In 1907, he entered Teachers College, Columbia University, to pursue further his interests in the teaching of ancient and modern languages. Four years later, however, Inglis emerged from Teachers College as a progressive experimentalist. According to one of his students, Inglis spent the remainder of his career repudiating his academic traditionalist formative years. His historical study of the development of the high school in Massachusetts, prepared as his dissertation at Teachers College, reflects the progressive style of historical research and to this day is employed by historians of nineteenth-century American education. He advocated the comprehensive high school not only in *Principles of Secondary Education*, but also as a member of the Commission on the Reorganization of Secondary Education. He participated in or directed nine school surveys and constructed Latin and English vocabulary tests, as well as intelligence quotient scales. Several of his books remained in print into the 1960s. Inglis traversed influential professional networks of the day, including the Cleveland Conference. A fine-grained profile of Inglis's career seems warranted.[4]

This book reports the results of an attempt to reconstruct the career of Alexander James Inglis in the context of historical interpretations of early twentieth-century education reform and of the progressive era. Organized along the trajectory of Inglis's career, it largely, though not exclusively, recounts his work chronologically. When appropriate, the study couches Inglis's work in interpretations not only of the progressive era and education reform writ large, but also of specific dimensions of those historical developments, including high school reform, the survey movement, testing, Latin pedagogy, and the institutions at which he worked. The focus, however, remains on ideas and practices endorsed and enacted by Inglis.

Because information about Inglis's life outside of his work is scant—no diary, journal, or personal reflections, no interviews with contemporaries survive, and the few available assessments of his personal qualities are connected mainly to his memorial service at Harvard—this book does not present, to use Oakes's term, a "pure biography" of Inglis.[5] Although, following Oakes's categories, this book perhaps best resembles a combination of "critical biography" and "scholarly chronicle," hopefully it presents something more than sheer critique and "straightforward recitation of facts." Because it attempts to explain Inglis's professional work in the contexts of education reform during the early twentieth century and of subsequent historical scholarship about the era, this study is perhaps better characterized as a *lifework history*, which may be defined as a systematic reconstruction and interpretive representation of an individual's lifework. When the lack of pertinent sources prevents definitive explanations of Inglis's actions, an attempt is made to offer explanations that, although speculative, seem reasonable in light of available documentation and the historic context. It is hoped that this study will illuminate not only Inglis's lifework, but also the principles and practices of education reform characteristic of the progressive era.

Inglis's lifework indeed manifests quintessential characteristics of the progressive era in American history. His career intersected with key developments in American education during the early twentieth century. Like any influential historical actor, Inglis was a product of his time and also contributed to his time. His participation in the developments of his era, however, frequently defies easy characterization—although aspects of his work resembled the overall contours that historians have identified for these developments, in important ways his work also departed from prevailing trends. The anomalies that emerge from his work not only reveal his career as in some ways unique and even pioneering, but also raise questions about the current historical interpretations of his era. In what follows, a brief summary of several important attempts to explain early twentieth-century American education precedes a detailed reconstruction of Inglis's career. The book closes with an assessment of the utility of these interpretations for explaining Inglis's career, a discussion of the implications of the record of Inglis's work for understanding the period and its prevailing interpretations, and a consideration of the role of biography in historical research.

Because Inglis was interested in aspects of secondary education that, at the time of this writing, again are prominent issues of education reform, including the organization of secondary education, the place of academic subjects in the curriculum, access to the curriculum, and assessment, it may be productive to consider the extent to which his work can inform contemporary school improvement efforts. Of course, any attempt to apply a practice from the past to present circumstances must consider not only similarities, but also differences, between historical contexts.

Explaining Early Twentieth-Century Education Reform

Educational and curriculum historians have evoked at least four interpretations to explain Inglis's era: Cremin's revolution in secondary education thesis, Krug's and others' social efficiency–social control thesis, Tyack's category scheme featuring administrative progressives and pedagogical progressives, and Kliebard's status politics thesis. Let us briefly consider each interpretation.

Cremin, in his discussion of the early twentieth-century "revolution in American secondary education," noted that "[t]he quarter-century between 1893 and 1918 was an extraordinarily creative one in American educational history."[6] The Committee of Ten report stood at one end of this era and the *Cardinal Principles* report at the other. According to Cremin, each report typified the prevailing conception of secondary education in its day. The contrasts that existed between these influential reports represented the "revolution in American secondary education" that occurred during the intervening years. Cremin summarized these changes as follows:

> From an institution conceived for the few, the high school became an institution conceived for all. From an adjunct to the college, the high school became the pivotal point in the public school system, one which carried forth objectives yet unfinished by the elementary school and opened new vistas leading on to the college. And from an institution restrictively concerned with the intellectual, the high school became an agency with no less a goal than the progressive amelioration of every individual and social need.[7]

Cremin's thesis has largely been eclipsed by Edward Krug's assertion that a commitment to the doctrine of social efficiency defined the age. According to Krug, social efficiency embodied promotion of both social service and social control, but emphasized the latter. For Krug, social control was "the management, and even the restraint, of individual behavior on behalf of the group." Krug defined "education for social control" as "the production of habits and beliefs consistent with desired kinds of behavior."[8] Krug saw social efficiency–social control doctrine manifest in many aspects of early twentieth-century education, including industrial education and, significantly for Inglis's case, the comprehensive high school.

Tyack's subsequent category scheme, featuring "administrative progressives" and "pedagogical progressives," extended and added nuance to Krug's concept of the social efficiency–social control doctrine. According to Tyack, administrative progressives "focused upon differentiating the structure and fulfilling the goals of social efficiency and social control" through the system of public education. Echoing Krug's language, Tyack asserted that administrative progressives were "primarily concerned with organizational behavior and the linkage of the school and external control, with aggregate goals rather than development of individual students." For Tyack, administrative progressives "constituted a political-educational movement with an elitist philosophy and constituency."[9] Pedagogical progressives, however, "spoke about the 'project method,' the 'activity curriculum,' and other ways to 'meet individual needs' of children by subverting the hegemony of established school subjects."[10] On the secondary level, such efforts took the form of ability grouping and curriculum differentiation. Although historians have tended to devote more attention and criticism to administrative progressives, even the efforts of pedagogical progressives to individualize educational experiences are depicted as part of a wider effort to fit students into the existing social order in ways that would serve class and capitalist interests.[11] Although Tyack's conception of pedagogical progressives is probably too encompassing to allow for distinctions among pedagogical progressives themselves, it is useful for distinguishing the priorities of that group from those of the administrative progressives (recognizing also that these two groups shared many priorities).

A fourth explanation of this and other periods is found in the application of the concept of status politics to the arena of curriculum reform. Kliebard explained: "In the context of status politics, conflicts revolve around the question of whose cherished beliefs shall be sanctioned, officially or otherwise." The struggle, then, "is primarily a symbolic one over whose most fundamental beliefs shall occupy center stage in a continuing drama."[12] Kliebard stressed that the validity of the status politics thesis to explain a particular curriculum reform does not necessarily detract from instrumentalist priorities that sought actually to change educational conditions. He continued,

> There can hardly be any doubt that key actors on the national scene like Harris, Bobbitt, Hall, and Counts wanted their proposed reforms to reach into classrooms and thereby to realize the social purposes that lay behind them. In many instances, they labored mightily to accomplish just that; but they were also fighting to have their treasured social beliefs and values endorsed through acceptance into the national debate over the American curriculum.[13]

In short, Kliebard concluded, "In the context of status politics, then, the curriculum in any time and place becomes the site of a battleground where the fight is over whose values and beliefs will achieve legitimation and the respect that acceptance into the national discourse provides."[14]

To what extent do these four interpretations of progressive era education reform explain Inglis's career? To what extent does Inglis's career inform these interpretations and our understanding of the era? We shall see, among other things, that Inglis's early educational transformation, continually widening professional interests, and intellectual method involved a repudiation of previously held cherished beliefs, that professionally Inglis personified Cremin's revolution in secondary education thesis, that for Inglis social efficiency meant providing students access to the curriculum and to life chances regardless of cost, and that although nuances in Inglis's work defy strictly categorizing him as either administrative progressive or pedagogical progressive, his work resembles the latter more than the former. The fine-grained perspective that biographical forms of research offer can complement and also problematize generalized interpretations of the past.

CHAPTER ONE

Young Latinist

Alexander James Inglis dedicated his formative years and his early career to the pursuit of an education largely consistent of the recommendations of the National Education Association's Committee of Ten. Between 1898 and 1908, he completed the classical courses at Middletown High School and Wesleyan University and embarked on a successful career as a Latin teacher, coauthoring three textbooks and preparing a translation of Cicero's *Essay on Friendship*. His commitments, however, clearly lay on the pedagogical rather than the philological side of classical scholarship. Before long, Inglis's interest in pedagogy would lead him to a near repudiation of his educational commitment to the classics.

In the spring of 1896, the Middletown City School District celebrated the opening of a new building for its high school. Residents of Middletown could boast that theirs was one of the oldest, if not the oldest high school in Connecticut.[1] On 26 March 1896, they could also boast that their new high school building featured the latest available physical and educational amenities. A gas engine drove the huge fan that powered the ventilation system; a nonexplosive boiler supplemented the ventilation system with steam heat during cold weather; modern plumbing adorned the washrooms; an electric circuit synchronized clocks throughout the building. Five classrooms, each connected with its own recitation room, an assembly room, drawing room, two recreation rooms, library, and chemistry and physics laboratories connected by a lecture hall, provided ample state-of-the-art space for teaching and learning. Constructed on the exterior of brown freestone, Potsdam red sandstone, Pompeian mottled brick, gray terracotta, and slate roofing with copper drainage fixtures, the two-story Romanesque-styled building served as a fitting edifice for the education of Middletown's youth.[2]

At the dedication of the building, William T. Elmer, president of the Board of Education, reported that during the previous nine years, high school enrollments in Middletown doubled to over two hundred students, attendance rates increased from 91 to 95 percent, the number of graduates increased by 300 percent, and the number of graduates continuing their education in college increased by 400 percent.[3] William North Rice, professor of geology at the nearby Wesleyan

University, delivered a lengthy address that placed the new building and the history of education in Middletown squarely in the context of "the democratic spirit of the modern High School."[4] He cited first the inclusion of girls and then the extension of education from the privileged classes to all classes of citizens as notable manifestations of this democratic spirit in American education. In stark contrast to the traditional "sharp distinction of castes in the matter of education," Rice claimed that the modern high school "tends to diffuse education, so far as it may be practicable, through all ranks of the community, and so to abolish the old sharp distinction between the educated and the uneducated." Rice regarded the modern democratized high school as "the People's College."[5]

Sophomore Alexander James Inglis likely attended this community event. On 24 November 1879, he was born into the third generation of Scots immigrants whose forebears twenty-seven years earlier had migrated from Edinburgh to Middletown, Connecticut. There his grandfather, Alexander Inglis (1815–93), had worked the local quarries. His father, William Grey Inglis (1854–1939), worked in a local gold and silver plating factory for thirty years before becoming proprietor of the Forest City Steam Laundry. A well-known family in Middletown, during the 1890s the local directory listed about a dozen Inglises, by reports all Republicans. Euphemia Inglis, for example, Alexander's first cousin, taught sixth grade at Central School; his uncle James Inglis served as superintendent of the bank burglar alarm system; another uncle Alexander W. Inglis was chief of police. Little information exists, however, about Alexander's childhood. In 1892, a visit to the parents of his mother, Susan Beyer Inglis (1858–1914), in Newark, New Jersey, turned tragic when Alexander's six-year-old brother Willie contracted diphtheria and died. If a memoir by a noted Middletownian is accurate, as he approached adolescence young Alexander likely sought relief from the summer heat by snitching chips from the ice wagon, and entertained himself by observing the arrival of the night riverboat on its journey from New York to Hartford on the Connecticut River or by witnessing the clamorous spectacle of the evening drill at the local firehouse.[6] What is clear, however, is that Inglis excelled in school.

The last three decades of the nineteenth century represent a period of transition and growth for public high schools in the United States. The transition from the academy to public high school, which began in 1821 with the founding of the English High School in Boston, was essentially completed during this period. By this time, fully tax-supported high schools were established, and public high schools and private academies, the former usually in cities and the latter largely in the northeast, comprised the two principal forms of secondary education. Although variation among public high schools continued, Middletown High School was probably typical. Nationally, enrollments in grades nine through twelve increased from about 80,000 in 1869–70 to 110,000 in 1879–80, 203,000 in 1889–90, and

511,000 in 1899–1900. In 1869–70 high school graduates represented about 2 percent of the population of seventeen-year-olds; in 1879–80 this figure increased to 2.5 percent. In 1889–90 secondary school enrollments equaled about 5.6 percent of the fourteen–seventeen-year-old population and high school graduates equaled about 3.5 percent of seventeen-year-olds. By 1899–1900, the equivalent of 10.2 percent of fourteen–seventeen-year-olds enrolled in secondary schools and the equivalent of 6.4 percent of the seventeen-year-old population graduated from high school.[7] Given these figures, the popular term "people's college" was something of a misnomer, at least from the perspective of any subsequent era. Although the number and proportion of adolescents attending and completing high school during this period increased, a secondary education remained beyond the reach of over 90 percent of the adolescent population. As Krug put it, during this period, "It was a rare thing to go to high school."[8] During the late nineteenth century, the American high school was an exclusive, elite institution that accommodated only some of the people's children.

At this time, local control of high schools resulted in sufficient variation in curricula that colleges were not assured of the adequate preparation of incoming students. Even the prevalence of admission examinations for both high school and college did little to mitigate the range of courses that students completed in high school. In 1892, the National Education Association charged a Committee of Ten with the task of recommending college entrance requirements intended to bring standardization both to college entrance requirements and to high school curricula around the country. Led by Charles W. Eliot, president of Harvard University, the Committee of Ten endorsed nine subject areas to comprise the college preparatory curriculum: Latin; Greek; English; other modern languages; mathematics; physics, astronomy, and chemistry; natural history; history, civil government, and political economy; and geography. Embracing the theory of mental discipline, which held essentially that the mind is like a muscle that could be strengthened through disciplined, rigorous study, for which some subjects were better suited than others, the committee endorsed these subjects in the order of decreasing disciplinary value. The committee insisted that all subjects should be taught the same way for all pupils.

The committee organized different combinations of these subjects into four courses of study: classical; Latin scientific; modern languages, and English. It considered the first two courses superior to the last two, but recognized completion of any of the four courses as representing adequate preparation for college admission. Although the express purpose of the committee was to standardize college preparatory programs and college entrance requirements, it maintained that college preparation was not the sole purpose of high schools. The committee asserted that successful completion of any of the four courses was also the best preparation for life. Reflecting contemporary enrollments and popular attitudes about education, the committee claimed, "Their [high schools'] main function is to prepare for the duties of life that small proportion of all children in the country—a proportion small in number, but very important to the welfare of the nation—who show themselves ready to profit by an education prolonged to the eighteenth year, and whose parents are able to support them while they remain so long in school."[9] The Committee of Ten endorsed an educationally elite curriculum for a demographically exclusive student body.

The period spanning the late nineteenth century and the early twentieth century was a difficult and uncertain time for classicists. Winterer indicated that "in the last third of the nineteenth century, the classical world quite rapidly receded from its important position in American intellectual and civic life, pooling instead in the esoteric byways of elite, high culture."[10] In higher education, classicists, who had long argued that the value of their discipline resided in its unique ability to impart cultural and moral values to students, responded to the rise of specialized research with new archeological inquiry through, for example, the American School of Classical Studies in Athens. Winterer maintained that, in fact, although they resisted arguments for increased utility of higher education, classicists embraced both general culture and specialized research as values of the classics—a commitment Winterer termed "cultivated erudition."[11] In the long run, the inexorable trend toward specialized research would ultimately undermine cultivated erudition.

On the secondary level, although enrollment in Latin as a percentage of all high school enrollments would not peak until the first decade of the twentieth century, classicists had felt their discipline under siege as early as the 1890s. The Committee of Ten, for example, not only recommended that the high school curriculum accommodate new subjects, especially science, but also dedicated less time to the study of classics. Of the four courses of study that the committee endorsed, only two included Latin and one Greek. Moreover, the committee recommended only two years of Greek and only four days per week of Latin study. Classicists responded to this affront with the formation of the American Philological Association's Committee of Twelve, which advocated among other things three years of Greek and five days per week of Latin study. Krug captured the sentiment of many classicists at the time, observing, "They felt like a beleaguered host defending the citadel of traditional culture against the onslaught of barbarians."[12] Their subject historically having occupied a preeminent place in the secondary curriculum, its hegemonic position was increasingly questioned.

A year-and-a-half after the release of the Committee of Ten's report, Inglis enrolled in the classical course at Middletown High School. Following 1865, the classical course at Middletown High School, designed to prepare students for college work, comprised the following: First year: Arithmetic, Algebra, Latin, Greek, Science; Second year: Caesar, Algebra, Latin, Physical Geography; Third year: Geometry, Cicero, Virgil, Xenophon; Fourth year: Review of Math, Algebra, and Geometry, Virgil, Homer.[13] In the 1898 annual report of the Middletown Board of Education, Superintendent Walter B. Ferguson expressed interest in "strengthening" the study of history at Middletown High School. "At present," he noted, "this subject is required of only those preparing for college, and they take merely Grecian and Roman history, and that for only a few months."[14] Inglis pursued a high school course of study that was strikingly similar to the classical course prescribed by the Committee of Ten.

In addition to offering a substantive curriculum, Middletown High School employed teachers who, by the standard of the day, were highly qualified: Albert J. Lonney and Elizabeth B. Fowler, Inglis's Latin and Greek teachers, respectively, both possessed a B.A. degree. Moreover, with respect to the classics, something of a spirit of educational innovation evidently imbued Middletown High School. Superintendent Ferguson, a graduate of Yale University, harbored a particular fondness for the classics, as he described to the Board of Education in his 1897 annual report:

> I am a firm believer in the great value of classical studies as a means for effective training in the use of correct English, in analytic and synthetic thinking, and as a means for arousing interest in peoples and civilizations that have contributed much to our own. I believe Latin should be retained in the high school curriculum, but I am sure many pupils who attempt the study could devote their time and attention more profitably to other subjects.[15]

Although he clearly felt that classical studies were not for everyone, Ferguson's faith in the classics was such that during the 1895–6 academic year he modified the curriculum to introduce the study of Latin earlier, in the "highest grammar grade," apparently the eighth grade. Beginning the study of Latin earlier in this way was, in fact, consistent with contemporary recommendations from both the Latin Conference of the Committee of Ten and the Committee of Twelve of the American Philological Association.[16]

Thus, in high school Inglis experienced a comprehensive classics curriculum taught by qualified teachers in a climate of innovation fostered by an enthusiastic educational leader—conditions conducive to inspiring any fledgling Latinist. He played football and probably baseball as well. In 1898, two years after the dedication of Middletown's new high school, Inglis graduated as one of the two students out of a graduating class of thirty-three who completed the classical course. He earned honors for perfect attendance during his senior year and first honors for academic achievement.[17] At the graduation exercises held on the afternoon of 24 June 1898, eighteen-year-old Alexander James Inglis, grandson of a quarryman and son of a launderer, delivered a short speech in which he argued for an end to American isolationism and the pursuit of enlightened alliances with other nations.[18] Inglis was about to embark on a career that owed much to the "democratic spirit of the modern high school" about which Professor Rice spoke two years ago. Inglis would become a leading proponent of the new American secondary education and would contribute to educational scholarship and practice in ways that outlived his tragically short career. Meanwhile, however, Inglis would immerse himself in further study of the classics.

During the 1890s, most prospective students qualified for admission to Wesleyan University by sitting for written examinations evaluated by members of the faculty. Admission to the classical course during the 1898 fall term required examinations in Latin (grammar, Caesar, Cicero, Virgil, "translation at sight into English of passages of Latin," and "translation into Latin of simple English"), Greek (grammar, similar translation requirements as for Latin, Xenophon, Homer), Ancient History and Geography, Mathematics (algebra, plane geometry), and English (exposition upon selected British and American works).[19] Admission by certificate was reserved only for graduates of Methodist academies and of Middletown High School. Inglis's Wesleyan transcript indicates that his only "Entrance Conditions" involved passing exams in Roman History, Greek History, and Ancient Geography. Despite Superintendent Ferguson's concerns about inadequate preparation in these subjects, Inglis passed the entrance exams.[20]

In the fall of 1898, Inglis enrolled at Wesleyan University in the midst of a period of significant institutional change. Inglis was among the public high school graduates who, though comprising only about one-fifth of Wesleyan students in the 1880s, by 1910 accounted for two-thirds of the student body. During the late nineteenth century, the Wesleyan faculty developed "a decidedly more scholarly and less denominational orientation."[21] The hiring of faculty with newly minted Ph.D.s and their increased involvement in emerging scholarly associations contributed to a new focus on scientific research and academic integrity. Inglis's college years also were a time of expansion and improvement in intercollegiate sports for Wesleyan. In 1899, Wesleyan formed the Triangular League with Amherst and Williams colleges to promote intercollegiate football and inaugurated championship competition in baseball and track as well.[22] Inglis distinguished himself at Wesleyan both through his scholarship and his athletic accomplishments and apparently worked part time to support himself. In addition to his studies, Inglis played varsity football and baseball each for four years. In baseball he played the position of catcher; during his senior year season he attained a batting average

Figure 1.1. Wesleyan football team, 1899. *Bottom row, second from left*: Alexander Inglis. Courtesy of Wesleyan University Library, Special Collections and Archives.

of .315. In football, during his third year he earned a place as substitute fullback on the All American Team; the next year he served as varsity football captain.[23]

Wesleyan offered three courses of study to its students: classical, Latin scientific, and scientific. The increasingly scientific orientation of faculty research was reflected in an increasingly flexible course of studies for students. Less emphasis fell on classical studies, allowing students greater choice of and access to emerging scientific studies. Although the emerging commitment to knowledge production, which is characteristic of many American campuses during the late nineteenth century, did manifest itself at Wesleyan, Inglis's experience was more consistent with the established collegiate tradition. Inglis focused his academic energies on the classics. His study of science was limited to a single course in chemistry, of social sciences to a course each in psychology and economics. Aside from four credits in mathematics and the requisite course work in declaration, declamation, composition, and rhetoricals, Inglis's course work outside the classics comprised six credits in German and two credits in Italian. The bulk of Inglis's course work was in Latin, Greek, and philosophy.[24]

Inglis completed philosophy courses in Logic, Advanced Logic, Introduction to Philosophy, Ancient and Medieval Philosophy, Modern Philosophy from the

Renaissance to Kant, and Modern Philosophy from Kant to the Present Time, as well as courses in Ethics and Evidences of Christianity through the religion department. Inglis's course work in Greek included selected reading of Lysias, Herodotus, Plato, and Homer, Demosthenes, Sophocles, and Plutarch, Life and Languages of the Greeks, Greek Comedy and Tragedy, and selected reading of Pindar and Bacchylides. During his senior year, he enrolled in a Seminary for the Study of Greek Archeology for no credit.

Inglis's course work in Latin ranged from selected reading of Livy, Terence, Plautus, Cicero, Tacitus, and of Roman Poetry to Latin Prose Composition and Latin Epigraphy, to Latin Paleography and Criticism, Roman Topography and Public Buildings, and Selected Chapters of Roman Archeology. During his junior year he enrolled in Roman Private Life and Social Institutions for no credit. The 1899–1900 midyear examination for Latin II, Cicero—Selected Letters indicates the academic expectations that Inglis grew accustomed to meeting. In addition to translating from Latin to English two passages of approximately two hundred words each and responding to questions of comprehension and grammar, as well as translating half-a-dozen sentences and phrases, the exam included the following exercises in English:

1. Give some account of the political purposes and actions of Cicero from the close of his consulship to his exile.
2. Give an outline of the correspondence between Cicero and Cato on the topic of a triumph for the former's victories in Cilicia.
3. State Cicero's attitude toward the quarrel between Caesar and Pompey, and his reasons for wavering in the matter of his ultimate allegiance.
4. Give the substance of Cicero's letter to Matius in the summer after Caesar's death, and of the reply of Matius.[25]

The last question on the exam was as follows:

8. Date your paper (8 Feb. 1900) according to the Roman reckoning;, and give a brief account of the changes introduced into the Roman calendar by Julius Caesar.

Inglis's linguistic talents were matched only by his athletic prowess; he evidently earned a reputation for both among his classmates. The 1901 Junior Personals in *The Olla Podrida*, Wesleyan's student yearbook, said of Inglis, "The first few weeks [of his life] were devoted to the art of kicking, in which he has since shown such proficiency. He could speak Latin fluently when a little past five, and he swallowed a long list of deponent verbs one day which caused his slight impediment of speech."[26] *The Olla Podrida* for his senior year included the following verse about Inglis: "He plays football and baseball and cards / He could punt, until hurt, sixty yards; / He talks Latin and Greek and can cuss like a streak, / And we give him our highest regards."[27] He apparently dabbled with the tenor banjo in his spare moments as well. During his senior year, Inglis served as delegate to the New York Alumni Banquet, as member of the Senior Ball Committee, as Class Day Marshall, and as class president. His fraternal memberships included Phi Beta Kappa, Delta Epsilon Kappa, and Skull and Serpent, the last a senior honor society founded at Wesleyan in 1867 with murky ties to Yale's more famous Skull and Bones Society. Despite these achievements, one wonders what social class bias Inglis may have experienced as, perhaps, his fraternity brothers had their shirts laundered locally by his father. Upon graduating, Inglis received the Wesleyan Phi Beta Kappa Prize in Latin.[28]

Inglis's four years at Wesleyan left him well prepared to assume his first professional position as teacher of Latin at the Kiskiminetas Springs School, a boarding school in Saltsburg, Pennsylvania. He taught there with a fellow graduate and baseball teammate from Wesleyan during the 1902–3 school year, also coaching football and assisting with the baseball team.[29]

His time at Kiskiminetas, however, proved brief. Although the details of his move remain obscure, during the summer of 1903, Inglis departed western

Figure 1.2. Kiskiminetas Springs School football team, 1902. *Second row from top, second from left*: Alexander Inglis. Courtesy of Alumni Affairs and Development, the Kiski School.

Pennsylvania for a position as Latin teacher at the Teachers College, Columbia University-affiliated Horace Mann School in Manhattan. He may have been attracted to the cosmopolitan milieu of Manhattan that he had experienced while at Wesleyan. Inglis taught high school Latin at the Horace Mann School from 1903 through the 1910–11 academic year. During Inglis's tenure, the Horace Mann School, although originally established for experimental purposes, largely served a college preparatory function for the select student body it attracted from the Manhattan environs. When the futility of practical experimentation became apparent, Horace Mann School came to be regarded instead as a "model school." As the historians of Teachers College put it, "in terms of the dominant educational philosophy of the day, as epitomized by the report of the National Education Association's Committee of Ten, it was a model school."[30] For the next half dozen years, Inglis devoted his professional energies to Latin instruction. During the summer of 1905, he studied at the American School of Classical Studies in Rome and also in Pompeii. Most significantly, during this period Inglis prepared three Latin textbooks. First, in 1904 his *Key to Pearson's Latin Prose Composition* appeared; in 1906 he coauthored the *First Book in Latin* with fellow teacher Virgil Prettyman; and in 1909 he coauthored the *High School Course in Latin Composition* with Charles McCoy Baker.[31] In 1907–8, Inglis and Prettyman's *First Book in Latin* replaced Bain's *First Book in Latin* on the Horace Mann School reading list. In 1909–10, the school adopted Baker and Inglis's *High School Course in Latin Composition*.[32]

Inglis and Prettyman's *First Book in Latin* employed the "grammar translation" approach to teaching Latin with brief readings and conversational exercises related to the content of particular lessons. The overall aim of the book was to prepare students to read Caesar. A reviewer writing in *The Classical Journal* expressed reservations about originating conversation in the exercises rather than in the teacher and about an apparent emphasis on composition, but otherwise recommended the book. The reviewer declared the book "an excellent example of the 'Beginning Book' now prevalent, the ordinary lesson containing some words, some forms, some syntax with explanation, Latin sentences to be translated into English, English to be translated into Latin, and an exercise on conversation."[33] Baker and Inglis designed the *High School Course in Latin Composition* to serve as the basis for three years of Latin composition study in high school, perhaps as a follow-up to Inglis and Prettyman's first year text. They presented a traditional and fairly rigid routine of drill and practice. They derived their vocabulary from Gonzales Lodge's study of Latin vocabulary for the high school and tied it to Caesar's *Commentaries* and Cicero's *Orations*.[34] Such instruction was wholly consistent with contemporary commitments to college preparation that dominated the Horace Mann School.

In addition to the three textbooks, during this time Inglis prepared a translation of Cicero's *Essay on Friendship*.[35] In the preface, Inglis claimed, "It is universality of application and of appeal which has made Cicero's essay on Friendship the cherished heritage of all ages, as valuable to us to-day as it was to the Roman of two thousand years ago."[36] Inglis supplied 118 notes to accompany the translation, which filled fifteen of the volume's eighty-three pages. The often cross-referenced notes typically provided detailed biographical and genealogical information for figures mentioned in the essay, as well as historical information and explanation. If it is true that "in modern American classical scholarship, footnotes often serve to prove the author's membership in a guild rather than to illuminate or support a certain point," then Inglis may have hoped his translation would signal his qualifications for membership in the classicist community.[37] Despite their sheer quantity, however, Inglis's notes rarely seem to offer more information than needed by the reader and certainly do not interfere with the text. Inglis demonstrated his mettle without excess.

Between his teaching and textbook writing, Inglis remained busy during his years at the Horace Mann School. During the 1906–7 school year, he also found the time to serve as director of the Horace Mann Mandolin Club.[38] During the late nineteenth century, the mandolin eclipsed the banjo as the most popular musical instrument in the United States. The craze for mandolin music began on 1 January 1880 when the Figaro Spanish Students debuted at New York's Booth's Theater. Although the Figaro Spanish Students actually played bandurias, not mandolins, their American imitators adapted the latter instrument to their orchestral style. Mandolin orchestras and ensembles became a prominent feature on the American musical landscape. The popularity of the mandolin peaked during the first decade of the twentieth century, just as Inglis advised the Horace Mann students. "Throughout the country, in towns and in colleges, mandolin enthusiasts formed amateur 'club' groups, typically ranging in size from quartets and quintets to larger ensembles of a dozen or more. Teachers organized their students into groups."[39] Two magazines made mandolin music available to these clubs, and lessons became available through private teachers and music stores. Although it is unclear whether Inglis played the mandolin himself—indications that in college he played the banjo perhaps suggest that he would be inclined to try his hand at the next popular stringed instrument—the prospect of a dozen students assembled in his classroom after school plucking out contemporary favorites such as "The Boston Ideal March" and "La Tipica" would present an amusing contrast to the staid Latin drills endured there earlier in the day.

As early as 1907–8, Inglis enrolled at Teachers College, Columbia University, for graduate work in education. That he chose to study education at Teachers College, rather than philology or archeology at Columbia University's, or the nearby Princeton University's, classics department, signals his commitment to the pedagogical side of the classics. He may have been attracted to further studies by Gonzales Lodge, who taught in and headed the language department at Horace Mann and also served on the faculty at Teachers College. Lodge earned his A.B. (1883) and Ph.D. (1886) at Johns Hopkins University, where he prepared his dissertation under Basil Lanneau Gildersleeve, the preeminent classicist in the United States during the late nineteenth century. After rounding out his studies in Germany and Greece, Lodge taught Greek at Davidson College and Latin at Bryn Mawr before becoming professor of Latin and Greek at Teachers College in 1900. Lodge also published several Latin textbooks, some coauthored with Gildersleeve.[40] Lodge was among the leading classical pedagogues in the United States during the early twentieth century. Inglis's initial interest at Teachers College appears unsurprisingly to have been in the area of Latin instruction.

During the 1907–8 academic year, Inglis took courses in History and Principles of Education with Paul Monroe and Practicum in Secondary Education with Julius Sachs.[41] Sachs received his bachelors and masters degrees from Columbia in 1867 and 1871, respectively. He studied at German universities and received his Ph.D. from Rostock in 1871. A year later he returned to the United States and established the Sachs Collegiate Institute for Boys in New York City. He served as headmaster there until he accepted an appointment at Teachers College in 1902. A classicist, Sachs published several studies of ancient literature and life. He served in 1890–1 as president of the American Philological Association and subsequently on the Latin conference of the Committee of Ten and on the Latin Auxiliary Committee of the American Philological Association.[42] He played a role in the establishment of the College Entrance Examination Board as well. Sach's background and interests, like Lodge's, probably resonated with Inglis. The paper that Inglis prepared for Sachs' practicum was published the following year in the *Teachers College Record.* Here Inglis suggested that the problem of an increasingly "crowded curriculum" in the secondary school could be resolved by providing for "closer correlation of the subjects of the curriculum."[43] Inglis focused on ways to correlate the teaching of foreign languages. Claiming to draw from language teaching practices popular at the time in Germany, he recommended that language teachers employ uniform terminology and that they identify appropriate aspects of different languages that could be transferred to the learning of other languages. Inglis provided numerous examples of the possibilities of these approaches in Latin, French, German, and English.

Within seven years of completing the classical course at Wesleyan University, Inglis had established himself as a classical pedagogue. He taught Latin at an elite private school, coauthored three Latin textbooks (at least one of which would remain in print into the 1960s), and prepared a translation of Cicero's

Essay on Friendship. Although in his translation of Cicero and summer study at the American Academy in Rome Inglis dabbled in philology and archeology, during this time he committed himself to the pedagogical side of the classics. Emblematic of Inglis's commitments or, as the status politics thesis would put it, of his "cherished beliefs," was Inglis's personal library of rare books, which included Charles Rollin's four volume *Ancient History*, published in 1827 in New York by George Long, John Clarke's *A Select Century of Corderius' Colloquies*, published in 1793 in London, Monsieur Fleury's *The History, Choice, and Method of Studies*, published in 1695 in London, and nine volumes of Cicero's collected works in Latin, printed in 1543 in Paris by Roberti Stephani (and bound during the nineteenth century).[44] Inglis's inscription in the first set indicates he acquired them during this period. Suffice it to say, the recommendations of the Committee of Ten were representative of Inglis's experience as a student and as a high school teacher. The next three years, however, would prove a pivotal time for Inglis, a time during which he put aside his work with Latin pedagogy in order to grapple with wider problems of secondary education.

CHAPTER TWO

Emerging Progressive

During the first decade of the twentieth century, Teachers College, Columbia University, and the Horace Mann School, not unlike Wesleyan University during the last decade of the previous century, experienced tremendous growth. Although Inglis's classical training at Wesleyan remained largely outside the main currents of scientific research that increasingly characterized American academe, such was not to be the case with his graduate studies at Teachers College. Although his initial interests at Teachers College continued to focus on Latin, in the intellectual milieu at Morningside Heights, Inglis could not remain untouched by new currents of educational theory and research. During the decade that Inglis spent at Teachers College, the systematic study of education as a professional field emerged propelled by the driving force of Dean James Earl Russell. Russell assembled a faculty whose scholarship and teaching contributed to the professionalization of educational studies and training in substantive and enduring ways. During Inglis's graduate study, for example, Edward L. Thorndike wrote his three-volume *Educational Psychology*, published in 1913; Paul Monroe edited the monumental five-volume *Cyclopedia of Education*, published between 1910 and 1913; and Julius Sachs addressed problems of secondary education in his 1912 work, *The American Secondary School and Some of Its Problems*.[1] These members of the Teachers College faculty, among others, taught Inglis. Again, it seems safe to suggest that Inglis's interest in the pedagogical side of the classics predisposed him to embrace aspects of the educational theory to which he was exposed while at Teachers College.

Between 1909 and 1914, Inglis fulfilled requirements for the M.A., prepared his dissertation, completed his Ph.D., served as acting principal at Horace Mann School and as assistant headmaster at the Belmont School, conducted his first school survey, and served as the first full-time education professor at Rutgers College. In the course of these professional activities, Inglis transformed himself from a Latinist, the quintessential academic traditionalist, to a progressive experimentalist. This stage of Inglis's career represents, in the words of John Lewis Gaddis, "a moment of sensitivity: some point at which small shifts at the beginning of a process produced large consequences at the end of it."[2] For Inglis, it marked the beginning of a professional transformation that personified the revolution in American secondary education that Cremin documented.[3]

The only record of Inglis's course work at Teachers College for the 1908–9 academic year is in the form of a final grade report for Education 212, Practicum in the Administration of Public Education in the United States, a year-long course taught by David Snedden and Samuel Dutton, pioneers in the field of educational administration, and offered through the Department of Educational Administration. In addition to this course, during that year Inglis fulfilled requirements for the M.A., degree with the completion of his masters paper, "Teachers Pension Systems in the United States: An Analysis and Criticism," which could have grown out of the practicum with Snedden and Dutton.[4] Inglis analyzed and rejected as insufficient two common arguments for teacher pension systems, philanthropy and reward for faithful services. He presented a detailed case that teacher pension systems increased the efficiency, that is, the effectiveness of a school system and identified criteria for a serviceable pension system for teachers. He devoted the bulk of his thesis to a critique of existing pension systems from around the country using the criteria he developed. This thesis is notable for its departure from Inglis's previous professional and academic work. Upon completion of his M.A., Inglis also received a diploma certifying him for service in school administration.

During the 1909–10 academic year, Inglis assumed a heavy course load that included Seminar in Secondary Education with Sachs; Educational Psychology with Thorndike; Practicum in Philosophy of Education with Professor McVannell of Columbia University's Philosophy Department; and Secondary Education in Germany, also with Sachs. No records document Inglis's work during the 1910–11 academic year, but he likely spent much of his time preparing his doctoral dissertation, which he completed that spring. Sachs, Monroe, and Gonzales Lodge served on Inglis's dissertation committee. Sachs appears to have been his major professor.[5] Under the influence of the Teachers College faculty, during the last two years of Inglis's graduate study, his professional interests shifted from focus on the problems of teaching Latin, to a wider view of pervasive problems of secondary education. Although Inglis never completely abandoned his interest in Latin, he devoted the rest of his career to wider problems of secondary education.

Inglis's doctoral dissertation manifests his shift in interest to wider problems of secondary education.[6] Here Inglis documented the emergence of the high school in Massachusetts prior to the Civil War. To prepare his study, he examined virtually every school report written in the municipalities of Massachusetts between 1838 and 1863, which numbered over five thousand. His largely descriptive study established the facts and identified wide trends in the history of high schools in Massachusetts. After tracing the roots of the high school to Latin Common Schools and Academies, Inglis reviewed the state legislation that impacted the development of high schools. He documented the establishment of individual high schools and discussed matters of noncompliance with state law, factors mitigating against the founding of high schools, and problems of defining what, exactly, qualified as a high school. He characterized legislation that failed to facilitate the establishment of high schools as "reactionary." Inglis examined the relationship between newly formed high schools and elementary schools and private academies. He regarded the exclusive concern of secondary schools with college preparation as "absurd," considering the small proportion of graduates pursuing higher education.[7]

Inglis devoted nearly half of his study to an examination of the changing high school curriculum. He reviewed high school admissions requirements. Relying on admittedly fragmentary evidence, he attempted to determine not only the subjects required by law, but also the subjects actually offered and the number of students who enrolled in them. He found that high schools frequently differentiated students by placing them in different "courses" or majors, that is, the English or general course and the classical course, by conducting these majors in separate departments, by maintaining separate departments for boys and girls, and by having separate schools for boys and girls.

In the longest chapter of his study, Inglis analyzed the content of the various subjects that comprised the high school curriculum in nineteenth century Massachusetts. Here perhaps is a glimpse of the beginning of Inglis's changing perspective on the school curriculum. He may have taken some pride to report that "Latin was one of the most extensively pursued subjects in the high school curriculum at all periods."[8] Inglis, however, did not hesitate to speculate about the reasons for the popularity of Latin despite decreasing value placed upon it by state legislation:

> The reasons for this are not far to be sought: 1. The prestige of the subject as intimated above; 2. The college admission requirements; 3. Scholastic inertia; 4. The machinery of school usage, the preparation of available teachers, the existence of a well established method, the presence of workable text-books–all these were factors which tended to conserve the subject as one of the chief studies for higher schools.[9]

Conspicuously absent from this list is any justification of Latin's continuing position of dominance in the curriculum on the grounds of its disciplinary or even educational value. At a time when defense of the classical curriculum was widespread and vigorous, Inglis, a champion of the Latin language and of its teaching, provided a reasonable account of the reasons for its popularity in the high school curriculum. Despite his vested professional and even financial interest in the place of Latin in the school curriculum, and despite the presence of two noted classicists on his dissertation committee, Inglis presented a disinterested discussion of its history. This posture signaled a change in Inglis's thinking about the curriculum; a repudiation of his early cherished beliefs had begun.

Despite frequent setbacks and its apparent limitations, Inglis regarded the emergence of the high school in Massachusetts as a favorable development. Consistent with the style of progressive history, he considered the expansion of the purposes and curricula of high schools and the opening of opportunities to increasing proportions of the population, especially to girls, as desirable, progressive developments.[10] In the final chapter of his study, Inglis placed the emergence of the high school in Massachusetts in the context of the rise of secondary education in the United States. He found commendable the fact that "no direct influence from other countries has been traced in regard to the high school system" that developed in Massachusetts. "The American high school," he concluded, "was an institution peculiarly adapted to the needs and wants of the American people and is an everlasting tribute to the democracy of Massachusetts and America."[11]

As if to crown his career at Teachers College, from 1 January 1911 until his resignation on 30 June 1911, Inglis served as acting principal of the Horace Mann School.[12] At the end of the spring semester, Teachers College awarded Inglis the Ph.D. His experience at Teachers College broadened his perspective and concerns from a microcurricular preoccupation with the teaching of Latin to a macrocurricular interest in the problems of secondary education in a democracy. Inglis had begun to move beyond the traditional academic commitments that had resonated with the recommendations of the Committee of Ten and had defined his early career.

That Inglis resigned from the Horace Mann School at the end of June 1911 suggests that by that time he had accepted the position of assistant headmaster at the Belmont School for Boys in Belmont, California. In 1885, William T. Reid, former president of the University of California, established the Belmont School as a semi-military boarding school having as its mission the preparation of its students for admission to elite colleges on the coasts. Belmont School offered the classical and English courses to its students as well as an aggressive program of interscholastic sports.[13] Following a summertime transcontinental relocation, Inglis assumed his responsibilities at Belmont during the fall term of 1911.

Documentation of Inglis's activities during his brief tenure at the Belmont School is scant. His duties as assistant headmaster apparently included the direction of athletics. That fall he was instrumental in hiring a coach for the newly formed rugby team. In his personal life, during the Christmas vacation Inglis married Antoinette Clark of Cortland, New York. The daughter of William H. Clark, editor and publisher of *The Cortland Standard*, one-time Cortland postmaster, and member of the New York Assembly in 1875, Antoinette studied at the Pratt Institute from 1898 to 1900 and at the Art Students League from 1900 to 1902, and illustrated children's books. Unable to travel across country to Cortland with adequate time for both a honeymoon and the return trip to campus, Alexander and Antoinette were married at the residence of Antoinette's uncle and aunt in Denver, Colorado. After a brief holiday in Colorado Springs, the Inglises returned to Belmont.[14] In the spring Alexander organized a fledgling baseball team, in which students initially lacked interest. In addition to his administrative duties, Inglis taught Latin and served as housemaster of a student residence.[15]

Inglis's background suited him to a headmastership and his reputation as a Latin teacher and textbook author may well have preceded him to the Belmont School. With nearly ten years of experience teaching Latin and his formal education completed at a prestigious Ivy League university, not to mention his success as an athlete, Inglis could easily have launched a career as headmaster and followed the circuit among elite college preparatory schools. Instead, at the end of his first year at Belmont, he resigned and returned to the east coast. During his graduate study at Teachers College, Inglis's interests broadened sufficiently to make school life less challenging to him. Although Inglis was on home turf in the prep school setting, he was also covering familiar ground.

Whether Inglis had arranged for long-term employment back east before he resigned from Belmont is unclear; that he engaged in short-term consulting

Figure 2.1. Alexander and Antoinette Inglis, date unknown. Courtesy of David M. Brooks. Collection of author.

is apparent. Between about 1910 and 1930, professors of education conducted over six hundred surveys of state, city, county, and municipal school systems throughout the United States. A survey could focus on a particular problem that a school system faced, or could entail a comprehensive analysis of an entire system. Historians writing during the late twentieth century generally depicted the survey movement as a manifestation of an early twentieth century commitment to the promotion of social efficiency and the establishment of social control through the agency of the school and viewed the survey movement as marked by an effort to impose business values on the public schools.[16] During the summer of 1912 the Westchester, New York, County Research Bureau secured Inglis's services to conduct a survey of school reports in the county. The survey represented an effort on the part of Westchester County school officials "to co-operate with the general movement... for increasing the efficiency of our immense and costly system of public schools."[17] This would be the first of nine surveys in which Inglis would participate.

The bureau charged Inglis with the task of assessing "the efficiency of the schools" in four areas: compliance with state compulsory attendance laws; student progress through the grades, that is, promotion and retention; graduation rates; and per pupil cost compared to other schools. Inglis complied with Westchester's desire for a statistical description of school activities. He analyzed data contained in official records and reports of school offices and county superintendents' offices, compared his findings to data available on a national scale, and compiled attractive tables and graphs to display his findings. Inglis even suggested simple formulas for arriving at what might be called an index of efficiency for each of the four areas of investigation. For example: "Efficiency in registration = Number of pupils of legal age registered/Number of children of legal age in the district minus number excused; Efficiency in preventing retardation [i.e., retention in grade] = Pupils of normal age plus pupils under age/Pupils in the school; Efficiency in progress through the grades = Number of pupils promoted/Number of pupils in the school."[18] Inglis was, however, dissatisfied with appearing to suggest that such a report provided a valid or even an accurate profile of educational activity in Westchester County. Indeed, Inglis expressed misgivings about the narrow notion of efficiency under which county officials operated.

Inglis cautioned his clients that the statistics prepared for state reports "do not correspond to administrative needs" of the schools. He suggested that to "gain the information requisite for a criterion of efficiency of schools, either the form in which the statistics are now gathered by the state authorities must be changed," or other kinds of information must be considered. He characterized information regularly used by teachers as "rich material" that could provide a fuller picture of education in Westchester County.[19] Inglis concluded his report by appealing to officials and citizens in Westchester County to embrace a wider definition of efficiency:

> There are several ways of promoting economy and efficiency. One is by saving money; another is by obtaining more or better service, or both, for the same money; a third is by increasing both the quality and quantity of service up to the full standard of service demanded by the citizen, even though the expenditure is therefore increased.
> To obtain less or poorer service than is paid for, to obtain less or poorer service than is needed, is waste.[20]

Inglis diplomatically advanced a conception of efficiency that went beyond conventional concerns about cost effectiveness. For Inglis, educational efficiency was a matter of providing students with the education they needed, regardless of cost.

During late spring of 1912, Rutgers College initiated a search for a candidate to fill a professorship for the science of education. Rutgers President William H. Demarest wrote to Teachers College President James E. Russell, requesting that he suggest potential candidates. Russell recommended several candidates, among them, Inglis. "Dr. Inglis wishes to get into college work and I think he is well worth considering," Russell wrote in reply to Demarest.[21] Following up on Russell's recommendation, Demarest sent one Professor Walter Marvin, who taught philosophy and psychology at Rutgers, to Teachers College to meet with the secretary of Teachers College's Appointments Committee, E. L. Thorndike. Of the half dozen contenders, Thorndike recommended Inglis most highly. His notes for Marvin stated, "Inglis—Very solid—tip top scholarship, sound sense—good manager—will get confidence of all teachers and state officers." Demarest promptly attempted to contact Inglis, but his telegram to Palo Alto, California, was reported undelivered, indicating that Inglis had already returned east. After inquiring of Russell and Thorndike for Inglis's address, Demarest finally reached Inglis through his father's address in Middletown, Connecticut.[22]

Rutgers College had not participated in the changes characteristic of American higher education during the late nineteenth century as had, for instance, Wesleyan University. Between the turn of the century and the Great War, however, New Jersey's land grant college instituted a number of reforms aimed at modernization. President Demarest led faculty in revising admissions requirements, converting from a quarter to semester calendar, replacing an elective system with "group" requirements, instituting requirements for majors and minors, and expanding academic programs. Curricular expansion occurred notably in agricultural programs, bolstered by federal funding for land grant institutions, and in education. In recent years, New Jersey had experienced a proliferation of new high schools accompanied by difficulty in securing qualified teachers, of which the state legislature now required a bachelor's degree. Rutgers responded to the need to prepare high school teachers by offering a new program in secondary education. This expansion of course work in education rendered the single part-time faculty appointment in education insufficient and resulted in the first full-time professorship of education, to which Alexander Inglis was appointed.[23]

President Demarest wasted little time in acting upon Thorndike's characterization of Inglis as a "good manager." Shortly after Inglis began teaching at Rutgers during the fall of 1912, he presented Demarest with a survey of the feasibility of making Rutgers Preparatory School a day school, a plan to publicize Rutgers' masters degree in education, a proposal to reorganize the courses in pedagogy, and a report on the work of the Committee on Extension work.[24] During the 1912–13 academic year Inglis taught Principles of Education and School Organization as well as Educational Psychology.[25]

In his proposal to reorganize the courses in pedagogy, Inglis noted that under the existing organization, topics were organized "haphazardly" and treated "superficially" in sprawling survey courses. He observed also that the "present organization is overburdened with theory and somewhat barren of application." After consulting with former professors of his at Teachers College, and with a new faculty member there, William H. Kilpatrick, Inglis proposed that during the junior year students study Principles and Organization of Education in addition to History of Education. During the senior year he would have them complement continued study of Principles and Organization of Education with in-depth examination of Educational Psychology, Secondary Education, Theory and Practice of Teaching, and Methods of Teaching before participating in Observation, Practice, and Practicum in Education during the spring semester. During 1913–14, with his proposals for reorganization largely accepted, Inglis taught Educational Psychology, Secondary Education, Principles of Education, Educational Sociology, and Educational Administration.[26]

In addition to his teaching duties, Inglis occasionally addressed faculty in area schools on the latest scientific educational research and assumed other responsibilities in the department and the college.[27] During 1914, Inglis served as Director of Summer Session for Rutgers College.[28] In this capacity, Inglis administered seventy-one courses, thirty-nine instructors, and over five hundred students. This work exposed Inglis to curricula in virtually every department in the college, ranging from Field Crops to Bacteriology to Costume Design to Integral Calculus to Beginning Zoology. That he engaged with issues in many of these curricula is indicated in the recommendations he offered for the next year's session. Much, though not all, of the Summer Session course work was geared toward teachers seeking to qualify for state certification. More indicative of the nature of professional education in the United States at the time, however, was the program of Extension Courses Rutgers offered during the school year for teachers.

Inglis chaired the Committee on Extension Courses during both of his academic years at Rutgers. The committee sought to make available for local schools "special lecturers and advisors in special fields of education from [the Rutgers] faculty and from other institutions who will deliver lectures, advise, and hold conferences on special problems of teaching before the teachers in various localities." For 1913–14, the committee organized four lecture series on "Educational Psychology—Adapted to the Needs of All," "Elementary School—Special Subjects," "General Principles of Education," and "Problems in Education." Extension courses in areas that paralleled the department's program and counted for degree and certification credit were also offered to teachers on Saturday mornings.[29]

The lectures in the series titled "Educational Psychology—Adapted to the Needs of All," provide a glimpse into the direction of educational studies at Rutgers. This series examined the following topics: the nature of education, instincts, association and habit formation, attention and interest, apperception, memory, mental discipline, and quantitative studies in educational psychology. In each case but one, laws or principles derived from scientific research were to be summarized and applications for the classroom suggested. Mental discipline would receive exceptional treatment, covering previous conceptions, psychological conception, experimental studies, and present day theories, but not classroom application.[30] Thorndike's influence on educational psychology, and on Inglis, was perhaps apparent here.

While at Rutgers, Inglis saw one article published. In it he attacked the problem of discrepancies among the most commonly cited figures for high school enrollment and graduation rates. The surveys he analyzed, those of Ayers, Strayer, Thorndike, and the U.S. Bureau of Education, were the same ones he employed for national comparisons in his study of the Westchester County schools. Analyzing existing surveys of high school enrollment, he established that the high school graduation rate for 1911 comprised about 31 percent of those students who had entered the ninth grade. Of those students who graduated, about half prepared for further education and about half immediately took up employment. He found that about one-third of those who graduated prepared for college and that about 15 percent prepared for other forms of postsecondary education. Inglis demonstrated that estimates of high school completion were typically unreliable and, more importantly from his perspective, that estimates of the number and proportion of high school graduates preparing for college were usually low. He noted that "[t]he number of high school pupils preparing for college and other higher institutions... is the largest homogeneous group in the public high school,"[31] but stopped short of exploring the implications of his findings.

As Inglis planned for the 1914 Summer Session at Rutgers, one of the original colonial colleges, the machinery of a faculty search geared up at the oldest of the colonial colleges. In 1892, Charles Eliot had established a faculty position in education within the Division of Philosophy at Harvard University. At the time, Eliot and most Harvard faculty regarded school reform chiefly as a means to improve the Harvard student body. Although Eliot supported such a faculty position, during the 1890s he was of a mind with faculty members who typically held that education was in no sense a specialized field of study but rather a service to provide to prospective teachers of prospective Harvard students. Paul Hanus, Harvard's first professor of education, struggled largely in vain to win the respect of the faculty of arts and science for the work he did. During the late 1890s, Hanus shifted his focus from teacher education to the training of administrators, though he never neglected the former responsibility. Suffering from status anxiety induced by the comparative advances in educational studies at other institutions, especially the University of Chicago and Teachers College, Columbia University, Hanus frequently lobbied Eliot for increased institutional and financial autonomy for the education program at Harvard. The success of these efforts finally was evidenced in the 1906 formation of a Division of Education independent of the Division of Philosophy.[32]

Hanus's success, however, was short lived. As A. Lawrence Lowell succeeded the retiring Charles Eliot in 1909, the latter's evolving support was replaced by the former's outright hostility to education as an area of systematic study. Conditions soon improved, however, as the rise of interest in the "science" of educational measurement lent academic credibility to educational studies. Both Lowell and Hanus came to regard the scientific approach to education as the best means for legitimizing the role of the Division of Education. The extent of Lowell's commitment to this development is best illustrated by his attempt, albeit unsuccessful, to lure to Harvard a recognized pioneer in the scientific study of education, E. L. Thorndike. During the first few years of Lowell's presidency, the school survey movement, a byproduct of both the scientific study of education movement and the popular notions about efficiency promulgated by Frederick Taylor, also impressed many university professors. Shortly thereafter, Harvard educational faculty embarked on an altogether new direction that emphasized the role of the school in achieving progressive social reforms.[33]

During the summer of 1914, Henry Wyman Holmes, the new chair of the Division of Education, approached Alexander Inglis about the possibility of his relocation to New England, to join the Harvard education faculty. Inglis's interest in the social role of the school demonstrated in his dissertation, his confidence in the promise of the scientific study of education evident in his work at Rutgers, and his early experience with the school survey movement in Westchester, NY, together suited him handsomely to the priorities at Harvard. That his former teacher (and fellow, but a few years senior, Wesleyan alumnus who had also completed the classical course) E. L. Thorndike again wrote favorably on his behalf, referring to Inglis, in short, as "just about the man you need," no doubt aided Inglis's cause, as well.[34]

Last minute problems with securing funding for Inglis's position temporarily delayed the search process. Then in mid-August Inglis visited Cambridge. On 29 August 1914 Inglis accepted the offer Harvard tendered him. Inglis's relocation was then delayed by a brief illness, for which Inglis apologized to the new division chair, noting, "For the first time in my life I have fallen into and escaped from the hands of a physician and this has interrupted my plans somewhat." In a subsequent reply to Holmes's expression of concern for his health, Inglis dismissed the diagnosis of food poisoning and assured Holmes that "[t]he harder the work the better and I was born to New England weather."[35] Inglis also advised Holmes of his interest in focusing his efforts on the problems of secondary education in his new position.

At Harvard, Inglis in effect conducted the program in secondary education. Initially, he taught courses in Principles of Secondary Education, [Secondary] Teaching, Historical and Comparative Study of Secondary Education, and a seminar in Problems of Secondary Education. A large portion of his teaching assignments were at Radcliffe College, from where a proportional part of his salary originated. Published course descriptions reveal that Inglis incorporated much of the material he taught at Rutgers into his Harvard courses, but with an exclusive focus on secondary education rather than on education in general. That virtually all of the topics and problems stated in the early course descriptions at Harvard appeared in chapters in his 1918 book, *Principles of Secondary Education*, is unsurprising; in the preface to the book Inglis noted that he had used the book in manuscript form in his teaching for several years prior to its publication.[36]

Within three years of earning his Ph.D. from Teachers College, Inglis had moved beyond his initial academic and professional commitments to Latin pedagogy toward an interest in wider problems of secondary education. Although Inglis's personal motivations for this transformation are not documented, it is likely that, at the very least, his experience at Teachers College primed him for broader challenges and responsibilities than continued work in Latin pedagogy or even secondary school administration promised. His inclination toward the pedagogical side of the classics, rather than the philological or archeological sides, may have predisposed Inglis to an interest in the educational theory he encountered at Teachers College. Or, perhaps through his professional reading, or through Lodge and Sachs, Inglis was aware of contemporary arguments for the place of the classics in the curriculum and found them less compelling, relying as they did on testimonials and rhetorical tactics more than on logic and evidence, than the rationale for the new educational theory professed by Thorndike and other progressives at Morningside Heights. If Inglis's subsequent proposals for education reform are any indication of his political beliefs, the conservatism that pervaded the community of classicists may even have prompted him to look elsewhere for an educational theory more politically palatable to him. Whatever the reasons—and, again, the absence of pertinent documentation prevents a definitive reckoning of his motivations—between the time of his initial enrollment in graduate study at Teachers College and his appointment to the Harvard faculty, Inglis had experienced an intellectual and professional transformation that would culminate in his participation in and contribution to definitive developments in the progressive education movement.[37]

In a provocative discussion of the nature of historical inquiry, John Lewis Gaddis applies concepts from the sciences to elucidate the historian's work. Several concepts that Gaddis employs in a discussion of biography seem to characterize nicely this stage of Inglis's career. Gaddis suggests "that in every instance in which historians have singled out one individual from masses of others, it's because there's been a moment of sensitivity." Gaddis defines this moment of sensitivity as "some point at which small shifts at the beginning of a process produced large consequences at the end of it."[38] This idea of "sensitive dependence on initial conditions," as Gaddis also puts it, may apply most appropriately to explaining the actions of individuals. It means that an individual was "in the right place at the right time," that the individual faced "a window of opportunity" that "could involve leaving the right things behind." Returning to scientific jargon, Gaddis summarizes by suggesting "that sensitive dependence in science almost always results from a phase transition: a point at which the properties of a substance are shifting to something else."[39]

How may Gaddis's insight apply to Inglis? For Inglis, his doctoral studies at Teachers College represented a moment of "sensitive dependence." He was entering a "phase transition" in which his "properties" were "shifting to something else." Exposure to the "new" science of education through study with Monroe, Thorndike, and others at Teachers College opened a window of opportunity for Inglis to head in a new direction. Rather than continue on the well-worn traditional academic path, which he rather easily could have done, Inglis began a transformation into a progressive experimentalist. The new perspectives Inglis gained from his doctoral work represented "small shifts at the beginning of a process" that eventually would result in "large consequences" for Inglis's career and for progressive education. These consequences would manifest themselves in the scholarship that Inglis had begun at Rutgers and would continue to pursue at Harvard.

CHAPTER THREE

Progressive Synthesizer

During the early twentieth century, the expansion and transformation of the high school in the United States outpaced the development of a systematic theory of secondary education. Although debates about the nature of secondary education occurred at the annual meetings of the National Education Association, in the pages of established and emerging professional journals and, as legislatures proposed various reforms for high schools, in the editorial and feature sections of general periodicals, a comprehensive synthesis of theory and research on secondary education was slow to materialize. Commentators of the day noted that books about the high school tended to present the narrow opinions of the author with benefit of a selective and by no means systematic review of the literature. Anthologies of viewpoints of "specialists," even when purportedly devoted to a particular approach to the high school, such as its social versus narrowly academic function, nevertheless provided nothing resembling a synthesis of theory and research on secondary education. Between 1914 and 1918, Inglis's initial considerations of the aspects of secondary education, including aims, college enrollment of graduates, reorganization of grade configurations, and the function of the junior high school, developed into a systematic examination of pertinent theory and research that culminated in the first comprehensive synthesis of thinking about secondary education, and became the model for such textbooks for decades.[1]

If Inglis had not already begun to study the problem of secondary education while at Rutgers, surely he launched this project immediately upon settling in Cambridge. Inglis's teaching assignment at Rutgers included a course about Secondary Education; at Harvard, Inglis taught Principles of Secondary Education, Historical and Comparative Study of Secondary Education, and Problems in Secondary Education.[2] During the first half of 1915, four articles he wrote on the high school were published. In January 1915, a book review he wrote appeared in *School and Society.* He reviewed two recently published books about secondary education, *The Principles of Secondary Education*, edited by his former teacher, Paul Monroe, and *The High School: Its Function, Organization and Administration* by John Elbert Stout. Inglis leveled sharp criticisms for both the books. He diplomatically but pointedly took Monroe to task for basing the concept of an anthology of writings about secondary education on the notion that the writing of a book presenting a comprehensive, unified theory of secondary education was too large a task for an individual author. Inglis found the views of specialists represented in the volume so diverse as to leave the immature student of secondary education in a state of confusion. He indicated a preference for additional material on the "aims and functions of secondary education" and on "criteria of subject values and aims." Inglis found Stout's book, on the other hand, strongest on the aims and functions of secondary education. He expressed disappointment, however, that Stout's book, offering neither references nor perspectives other than the author's, was dangerously biased. Inglis admonished: "A dogmatic statement may offer a stimulus to the student's thought; it seldom affords a basis for orienting that thought."[3]

Another publication that appeared that year in *School and Society* reiterated the point Inglis advanced in his 1913 article in the *Educational Review*. The 1915 version benefited from the consideration of census data not discussed in the earlier piece. In light of the new data, Inglis reasserted his initial conclusion that the number and proportion of high school graduates who continued their studies in college was larger than commonly acknowledged in educational discourse.[4]

Inglis's modus operandi was becoming apparent: illuminate an educational issue of the day by applying the best available evidence to the particular problem. A notable example of this kind of work is found in Inglis's 1915 discussion of "A Fundamental Problem in the Reorganization of the High School."[5] By this time, deliberation about the "reorganization" of secondary education—that is from the 8–4 grade arrangement to either the 6–6 or the 6–3–3 plans—was ubiquitous in the educational literature. Inglis approached this issue by examining extant theories and research on child development and available data on enrollment. He summarized both Hall's theory of "salutary development," which held that abrupt changes characterized the onset of adolescence, and Thorndike's theory of "gradual development." Next, Inglis surveyed studies of pubescence and maturation in boys and admitted that sufficient evidence existed to support a sharp differentiation of elementary and high school. He advised, however, against such a premature conclusion in light of evidence that development was more dispersed among the early adolescent years for girls and argued that any plans for coeducational high schools must take this reality into consideration. Inglis concluded that the overall range of development in grades seven, eight, and nine could not warrant abrupt transitions from elementary to secondary school. He examined further data and found that, typically, no more than one-third of students at a particular grade level were of the age considered appropriate for that grade, and also that the remaining two-thirds of students were widely dispersed above and below the corresponding chronological age for that grade. Inglis concluded that grades seven, eight, and nine "represent distinctly a transition stage and that the changes which are made [should] be undertaken with the intention of providing a gradual and continuous transition in which the conception of radical differences between elementary and secondary education plays no part."[6] For Inglis, the organization plan was of secondary importance to the imperative of providing students with "materials and methods" that enabled them to develop at a rate appropriate for them. The teaching of students in large groups necessitated gradual transitions from one grade level to the next.

In an article published in the May 1915 issue of *Teachers College Record*, Inglis articulated the core principles of his theory of secondary education that he would later elaborate in his 1918 book. He identified four "fundamental aims of secondary education," which he regarded as "the controlling aims of the American high school": the social-civic aim; the economic-vocational aim; the individualistic-avocational aim; and the physical aim.[7] He stressed that "they are by no means mutually exclusive aims: rather they are necessarily interrelated and interdependent."[8] In the context of the debate over the appropriate role and place of vocational education in the system of secondary education, Inglis cautioned, "[o]ver-emphasis on the economic-vocational aim to the partial neglect of the other aims is a not impossible danger at the present time."[9] For Inglis, collectively these four aims constituted the larger "social aim of secondary education." He emphasized, however, that the "socialization of the high school," that is, the reorganization of secondary education for the purpose of achieving the four aims, "is a perpetual problem arising out of the dynamic character of society."[10] He suggested that secondary education must undergo continual evaluation and revision in order always to contribute to working toward social ideals and improving social realities.

Inglis identified three factors that necessitated the continual reevaluation of secondary education. The first two factors were closely related: the "dynamic character of society" and the varying rate of change in society. Significantly, both of these factors pointed to, among other things, "the necessity of providing training [to students] for the development of a capacity to read just as well as for adjustment to the conditions which exist at any time."[11] Inglis asserted, "there is constant danger that we may tend to overemphasize adjustment to the neglect of the element of readjustment."[12]

The third factor that Inglis considered important was "the heterogeneity of the group which is to be socialized in part through the high school." Inglis held that a "certain degree of unity in feeling, in habit, in ideas, in conduct, in thought is a necessity of any form of society." He considered this necessity "greater in a democracy than in any other form of society."[13] Inglis suggested that the increasing diversity of American society and the corresponding need for unity held greatest implications for the social-civic and individualistic-avocational aims of secondary education. He proposed that two phases, or functions, of secondary education be provided through the educational program of the school in order that both of these aims are met: "integration" and "differentiation." He emphasized that to oppose integration and differentiation against each other was "fallacious" and that they were in fact "supplementary." Inglis claimed that "integration and differentiation must be conceived not as conflicting with each other but as supplementary phases of the same unitary process."[14] The differentiation and integration functions would serve as the cornerstone of Inglis's theory of secondary education.

Inglis's study of the problem of the "reorganization" of secondary education logically led him into the territory of the junior high school. He presented his thinking on this issue in two pieces published late in 1916.[15] Inglis promulgated three-dozen principles undergirding the idea and practice of the junior high school, which he classified into three categories. In his discussion of principles related to the nature of the pupil, he reiterated his position on the gradual and continual transition from grade level to grade level, from elementary school to junior high school to high school. Inglis called for what today would be referred to as developmentally appropriate classroom practices. In his discussion of principles related to the nature of society, Inglis reiterated the four aims of secondary education he advanced in 1915. Additionally, he articulated six "functions" of education that arise from the four aims: the integrating function, the differentiating function, the selective function, the adjustive function, the propaedeutic function, and the diagnostic function. He identified three ways that schools should be more efficient in the sense of better serving the needs of youth. In his discussion of principles related to the administration of school programs, Inglis called for, among many other things, increased school attendance, decreased retention in grade, better articulation with elementary and secondary education, and more social activities for students. Anticipating a pressing problem with junior high school curriculum, Inglis asserted that the "worst error we can make is to 'push down' into the seventh and eighth grades 'high school' subjects."[16]

Inglis's recommendations represent the more progressive vision of the junior high school, a vision that subsequently was lost, as many junior high schools became exactly that—junior versions of the high school with subject matter "pushed down" from later grades. Inglis portended that the suggestion that "the character of the junior high school be determined by the needs of those who go on to senior high school" would be "fatal to the success of our school system."[17] Inglis envisioned the junior high school occupying a unique and transitional place between the elementary and secondary education. This perspective held implications for curriculum and instruction. "Neither elementary school methods nor secondary school methods can be satisfactory here," he claimed.[18] He recommended that, in the transition from the experience of the self-contained classroom to the departmental organization, a plan for combining self-contained classroom organization with departmental organization would gradually increase the latter so that by the tenth grade it would appropriately predominate.

During the spring of 1915, Inglis negotiated with Ellwood Cubberley, general editor of the Riverside Textbooks in Education series, through Houghton Mifflin editor Franklin S. Hoyt to establish a series devoted to secondary education. In June, Houghton Mifflin executed a contract with Inglis. During the following autumn, Inglis proposed "Ideal Standards" for books under his editorship. At least one manuscript was initially rejected, then revised, and ultimately accepted when it conformed to Inglis's standards.[19] Before Inglis assumed these editorial responsibilities, however, Cubberley had invited David Snedden to prepare a manuscript on the general topic of secondary education. Discussion among Cubberley, Inglis, and Hoyt resulted in the decision to list Snedden's book under Inglis's series rather than Cubberley's. This decision seems to have been a matter of logical placement, since Inglis apparently had no editorial input to Snedden's manuscript. Snedden's book, *Problems of Secondary Education*, was published in 1917 and enjoyed brisk initial sales.[20]

From the start, Inglis had envisioned a textbook on the general principles of secondary education as the "keystone" to the secondary education series. He assumed this responsibility and by the beginning of the 1916 fall semester was in a position to estimate that his manuscript would be ready to go to press during the following January. During December 1916 he was beginning final revisions to his manuscript based upon feedback from critics he had selected.[21]

Correspondence between Inglis and his editor at Houghton Mifflin indicates that he was at work on the manuscript that would become *Principles of Secondary Education* as early as the fall of 1915. The October 1916 issue of *The Harvard Teacher's Association Leaflet* reported that Inglis had completed his book and that it would likely be available early the next year.[22] Inglis apparently submitted his manuscript by the start of the summer of 1917; Houghton Mifflin issued him a contract in mid-July. By that time, Inglis was securing permissions. He completed proofs of the graphs in September, figures and the preface in October, and page proofs in November 1917. *Principles of Secondary Education* was published in January 1918.[23]

Inglis elaborated many of the ideas he had articulated in his earlier articles in *Principles of Secondary Education*. He could well have written *Principles* as a follow-up to the criticisms he had advanced in the 1915 *School and Society* book review. Perhaps he had planned such a book prior to preparing the review.

He may even have been writing it by that time. In any event, Inglis devoted half of his preface to *Principles* to a brief consideration of the advantages and disadvantages of the multiauthor versus the sole author approach to a scholarly textbook and to delineating the measures he took to avoid the perils of myopic opinion and unsubstantiated claims. The latter involved employing specialized studies as evidence to support positions in the book and subjecting the manuscript to the review and recommendations of specialists.[24] Inglis clearly intended to set his book apart from others available at the time. He devoted the rest of the preface largely to a brief description of the organization of the book. Inglis divided *Principles* into three sections each corresponding to the three fundamental factors of education he had earlier identified: the nature of students, the ideals and realities of society, and the "means and materials" of education.[25] An overview of the highlights of each of these sections will illuminate the principles of secondary education Inglis advanced.

Inglis devoted part I of his treatise to a consideration of the bearing of the nature of the pupils on principles of secondary education. He dedicated separate chapters to physical and mental traits of pupils, individual differences among pupils, and a broad profile of the student population. Inglis's commitment to the application of the new scientific measurement to understanding educational problems suffuses this part of the book. Laden with tables and graphs, these chapters brim with data. Inglis's method was to lay out all of the extant theories and evidence he could procure, evaluate every finding and proposition, identify the conclusions best supported by the data, and suggest the implications of these conclusions for secondary education.

Portions of part I obviously grew out of Inglis's earlier articles published in 1915 and 1916. Often times he informed these discussions with additional data. He revisited, for example, evidence he had previously discussed about pubescence and maturation in boys and girls. Inglis concluded that for the purposes of administering schools, the segregation of boys and girls or both according to their point of physical development was inadvisable. After reviewing theories of mental development, he concluded "that the fundamental mental processes begin with the early years and continue throughout life without change so far as the mode of their operation is concerned."[26] Thus, Inglis rejected educational proposals that prescribed skill-drill exercises for children and higher order modes of thinking for youth, opting instead for a blend of the two throughout the school years and for gradually increasing abstract work with age and development. Inglis restated his commitment to the principle of gradual and continual transition of materials and methods of instruction throughout the grades of schooling, as well.

Inglis's positions on mental ability, or intelligence, represented what is best described as enlightened opinion in his day. He characterized mental differences between the sexes and between races as minimal and attributed those differences more to environmental factors than to factors of heredity:

> Such differences must be considered as contingent and not necessary results. Like treatment of boys and girls might well eliminate many sex differences now found which are the results of unlike treatment. This may or may not be desirable. This same principle also applies to many so-called racial differences. Doubtless many observable traits which we note in certain races in America are due solely or primarily to the social treatment to which they are subjected. Many of these secondary education should aim to eradicate.[27]

Inglis was writing during a time of profound ferment in American social science. Coben documented that "[p]robably the most significant achievement of academic intellectuals between 1912 and 1930 was their crucial role in the nearly complete repudiation of every scientific rationale for racism." Coben concluded, "As a result of the all but unanimous rejection of racism by the scholars most involved in the study of race, [these] ideas... became the conventional wisdom of intellectuals, insinuated by them throughout American society, especially through educational institutions and the higher courts."[28] Inglis struck this position early during the repudiation. Inglis wrote amidst persistent racism, sexism, and nativism, even among reformers, indeed at the very moment when D. W. Griffith's *The Birth of a Nation* was causing a national sensation with its racist themes.[29]

Finally, Inglis reiterated his discussion of the nature of the student population, indicating again that estimates of college-bound youth were generally inadvisably low. He identified the typically difficult transition from elementary school to high school as a probable cause of the large "elimination," or dropout, rate in the early years of secondary school. He identified three general categories of high school students, those completing high school, those dropping out during the second year, and those dropping out during the first year, and encouraged educators to provide for the educational needs of these groups according to their destinies, until "elimination" could be eradicated.

Inglis's confidence in statistical studies was tempered by acknowledgment of the limitations of educational measurement, which he probably learned from Thorndike. In his analyses of psychological theories and accumulated evidence, Inglis typically concurred with Thorndike. (On the other hand, Inglis frequently rejected the conclusions, as least those that related to secondary schooling, of another teacher, Paul Monroe.) Inglis approached statistics, however, with due caution. He wrote, for example, "one must be careful not to infer too much from averages which can hold true for large groups only and cannot be applied safely to individuals or small groups because of the great variability found." Despite his heavy reliance on psychological studies for the identification of educational principles, Inglis advised that "it may be said that no single psychological trait has ever been adequately measured and that the most painstaking investigations have failed to afford evidence which is entirely satisfactory." Inglis's confidence that such evidence would one day be available did not inflate his interpretation of available data. He warned his reader that "the statistical data presented must be considered as indicative of general tendencies rather than as exact and conclusive evidence as to details." Prudent warnings about the limitations of statistical studies framed Inglis's examination of the evidence.[30]

In part II of his book, Inglis examined secondary education from an institutional perspective. He traced its history in America, compared its organization and curriculum in Germany, France, and England, discussed its articulation with other levels of schooling, and considered its purposes in relation to the ideals of a democratic society. Inglis organized the historical development of secondary education in the new world into three overlapping phases: Latin grammar schools, the academy movement, and the rise of the public high school. He outlined the legal and institutional development of these forms of secondary education and discussed the high school's purposes and curriculum as reflections of changing social needs and conditions. That Inglis's historical account of the high school in the United States placed discernible emphasis on events in Massachusetts is unsurprising, considering not only his previous research on the subject, but also the influence of that state on secondary education in other parts of the country. Inglis's general stance on the rise of secondary education, particularly its expansion to all classes of society and especially to girls, echoed the positions he struck in his dissertation.

Inglis briefly described the development and organization of secondary education in Germany, France, and England. He devoted particular attention to the relationship between organization and curriculum and the social structure of each nation. He carefully articulated recognizable strengths and weaknesses of each system. Inglis cautioned the reader against fallacious comparisons of national education systems that failed to account for the peculiarities of social structure. He suggested that comparisons of the achievement of American students to students in European systems should be corrected for the more selective and exclusive character of the latter. Inglis stressed the greater reflection of social and economic status that operated in European systems, observing that European nations maintained what in effect were two or three parallel school systems.

Inglis devoted two chapters to consideration of the relationship of secondary education to elementary and higher education. He contended that the division of elementary and secondary education depended less on sound pedagogical principles than on arbitrary, largely administrative, considerations. He reiterated his work on the wide dispersal of ages and levels of maturity at a given grade level, calling again for gradual and continual articulation of materials and methods from elementary through secondary schools. Inglis also restated his position on the nature and function of the junior high school. Here he extended, slightly, his progressive stance on the curriculum when he recommended organizing the curriculum of the junior high school in terms of the nature of the students and their lives in society rather than according to the logical arrangement of subject matter.[31]

Inglis attributed the closer relationship of the secondary school with higher education than with the elementary school to the influence of European forms of education, which held the elementary school as appropriate for the lower classes and the secondary school as fitting preparation of the upper classes for university study. He noted that during the nineteenth century this arrangement was challenged, earlier in American than in Europe, by the notion that secondary education should serve wider purposes than preparation for college. Regarding this trend toward a broadening of the purposes of secondary education, he noted, "Its fulfillment in practice is as yet by no means complete."[32] Inglis examined numerous issues related to the relation of the school to college, including the rise of public state universities, late nineteenth-century efforts to lend uniformity to college entrance requirements through the certificate and examination approaches, and the organization of accrediting associations. He restated his findings on the number and proportion of high school graduates entering higher education, as well. Inglis observed that the dominance of college entrance requirements restricted the flexibility of the high school curriculum. He reviewed studies of the correlation of performance on college entrance examinations with performance in college course work and found that the results were, at best, mixed.

Inglis based his discussion of "social principles determining secondary education" on three assumptions: that society continually evolves, that the interests of the individual and of society complement each other, and that the school, "as a social institution," is "maintained by society for the purpose of assisting in the maintenance of its own stability and in the direction of its own progress."[33] The last of these assumptions led to a consideration of four principles of secondary education, which held that the high school should address social ideals and realities, should change in response to social changes, should foster both "integration and differentiation," and should not duplicate but rather complement functions performed by other social institutions.[34] Inglis emphasized, among other things, that the inexorable reality of constant change required that students not only be able to adjust to existing social conditions, but also possess the ability to readjust to unpredictable future circumstances. Additionally, he asserted that every society has at work within it two supplemental, complementary forces, one toward integration, the other toward differentiation. Inglis insisted that social institutions must provide for both of these forces in concert with each other. Here he obviously reiterated the principles he had articulated in his earlier publications.

After establishing these principles, Inglis contended that all social institutions should contribute to their attainment. Changes in some institutions, he claimed, would necessitate changes in others, including the institution of secondary education. He devoted the rest of the chapter to an elucidation of recent changes in the institutions of the family, community, religion, and industry. Inglis suggested general implications of these changes for secondary education, such as provisions for vocational education, attention to moral-social education, and the need for the school to foster "a certain amount of unity of thought, of feeling, of ideas, of standards, of conduct."[35]

In his elucidation of the aims and functions of secondary education, Inglis reiterated the principles he had advanced in his 1915 article on "the Socialization of the High School." He introduced this discussion by stipulating that the aims of secondary education should be based upon life activities. Inglis rejected, however, the possibility of arriving at a complete, detailed analysis of life activities. He proposed, instead, three general "fields of activity" that formed the three fundamental aims of education: the social-civic aim; the economic-vocational aim; and the individualistic-avocational aim. The social-civic aim "involves the preparation of individuals for efficient participation in those activities of society whose controlling purpose and primary object are desirable forms of social cooperation." The economic-vocational aim "involves the preparation of the individual for efficient participation in those activities of society whose controlling purpose and primary object involve economic efficiency." The individualistic-avocational aim "involves the preparation of the individual for those activities of life whose primary object and controlling purpose are personal development and personal happiness through worthy use of leisure." As he did elsewhere in the book, Inglis employed the term *efficiency* in the sense of *effectiveness*.[36]

Inglis articulated six subordinate functions of secondary education necessary for attaining the three aims. The "adjustive or adaptive function" would enable the student to adjust to current social realities as well as to adapt to changing realities in the future. The "integrating function" would promote social integration among an increasingly diverse population and was "supplemental rather than conflicting" with the "differentiating function," which would cultivate individual abilities and aptitudes "out of necessity of taking advantage of the differences among individuals for the purpose of determining social efficiency." The "propaedeutic function" involved "preparation for higher education," which Inglis suggested should be neither neglected nor overemphasized. Inglis argued that the "selective function" would operate not through elimination from programs at which a student had no talent, as was conventional practice, but through differentiation. This meant "that if a pupil lacks interest or ability in one field of study but possesses ability and interest in another, discrimination is justified, and, particularly in the public secondary school, that pupil has a right to receive education in fields for which he possesses ability and interest." For Inglis, the student "cannot be deprived of the opportunity for education because of inability or lack of interest in some officially favored subject or subjects." Finally, the "diagnostic and directive function" rested on the premise that "each individual, as far as may be possible, should do what he can best do." This meant that "the school must provide materials to acquaint the pupil with various activities of life, must give him some opportunity to test out and explore his capacities and interests, and must provide some direction and guidance therefore."[37]

Inglis presented the three aims and the six functions as "supplementary" and interactive. He attributed many problems of secondary education to a failure to pursue these aims and functions in relation to each other. Ultimately, the aims and functions of secondary education would inform the planning, organization, and implementation of the high school program.

Inglis devoted part III of his book to a discussion of the necessary impact of the aims and functions of secondary education on "the means and materials of secondary education." For Inglis, the place of each subject in the curriculum was determined by the extent to which that subject supported the achievement of the aims and functions of secondary education.[38] He asserted that subjects could have direct or indirect value in achieving the targeted aims and functions. By direct value Inglis meant that something learned in a subject could be directly applied to life activity. By indirect value Inglis referred to the deferred application of a particular learning. In American society, for example, facility with the English language held direct value, while facility with Latin held indirect value, at best. Inglis held subject matter with direct value in higher esteem than subject matter with indirect value. With respect to the latter, Inglis advocated the identification of subject matter that bore the greatest potential for later transfer. He reviewed extant psychological theories and studies of transfer of learning. Inglis rejected "faculty psychology" on a number of grounds, characterizing it as "relegated to the limbo of discarded absurdities."[39] He compared the theories of Judd and Thorndike, gleaning what he felt to be the most reasonable aspects of each, but relying more heavily on Thorndike's idea of "dissociation." Inglis explained this idea as applying to an element of subject matter that could be "dissociated" from exclusive application in its usual disciplinary context and thus applied elsewhere, though not as widely as subject matter with direct value. Inglis maintained that while such transfer was not spontaneous in most people, it could and should be taught to most people using the method promulgated by Thorndike.

After a brief historical overview of changing values, or priorities, attached to various subjects, Inglis noted the sheer logistical impossibility of all students studying all subjects. This reality pointed to the need to "select" the subjects to include in the secondary curriculum. He devoted the bulk of part III of *Principles* to a consideration of the relative value of each of the conventional subjects. For Inglis, the direct and indirect value of subject matter, as well as the extent to which a subject contributed to the achievement of the three aims and six functions of secondary education, served as important criteria in such a process of selection.

In a chapter devoted to "The Place of Foreign Languages in the Program of Studies," for example, Inglis specifically discussed the past, present, and prospective status of Latin in the high school curriculum. He summarized the arguments in support of including foreign languages in the curriculum, evaluating each language according to its direct and indirect value to the curriculum. Inglis thoroughly analyzed their direct and indirect values against logic and the best available evidence, concluding that the direct values claimed for foreign languages in the curriculum were "limited and contingent."[40] He concluded further that "the values of the study of Latin and Greek for purposes of social intercourse and for commercial purposes are *nil*," that "their vocational and instrumental values are limited to a few professions," and that the "social–cultural values of the study of the classical languages" are not only "less limited," but also overstated because the study of a culture and its literature was more efficient in the student's first language.[41] Inglis contradicted Senator Henry Cabot Lodge's recent contention that the theory of mental discipline, often evoked in defense of the classics, was universally accepted.[42]

Inglis allowed that the study of a foreign language could increase a student's vocabulary in his or her first language, but cautioned that this effect had been overstated. From this analysis, Inglis reasoned that, although difficult to justify against direct values, indirect values for foreign languages were sufficient to entitle them a place in the curriculum. Inglis concluded that, although the large proportion of students enrolled in foreign languages at the time was not justified in light of the limited direct value of such studies, the indirect values of such study warranted inclusion of foreign languages in the secondary school curriculum. Clearly, this conclusion represented a departure from Inglis's initial academic and professional commitments as an educator. Inglis rejected academic formalism, as well as the conventional practice of organizing curriculum around the logic of subject matter rather than around the needs and interests of the learner.[43] Inglis would return to these themes in both his survey work and his later writings about Latin in particular and secondary education in general.

Inglis dedicated the last two chapters of his book to the problem of viewing the secondary curriculum as a whole. He briefly reviewed historic organizations of the secondary curriculum from the Latin grammar school to the academy to the public high school. He devoted special attention to the recommendations of the report of the Committee of Ten. Inglis found these recommendations "open to serious criticism." He listed seven criticisms, implying that a complete analysis would yield others, including the following: neglect of vocational education, exaltation of the college preparatory curriculum, "differentiation of curriculums on the basis of predominant subjects rather than on the basis of the activities of life to which pupils will apply their training," excessive stress on foreign and ancient languages, lack of provision for students who leave high school before completing the course of study, relatively inflexible programs of study, and failure to accommodate individual differences.[44] Based on a consideration of the aims and functions of secondary education he identified earlier, Inglis instead recommended organizing the secondary school curriculum around "constants," subjects taken by all, and "variables," areas of the curriculum open to student election. Constants would be comprised of subjects of nearly "universal value" such as English, social science, health and physical education, general science, and music appreciation. Variables would be comprised of subjects that served a student's special interests and vocational aspirations. Inglis proposed that programs of study be sufficiently flexible to accommodate student growth and choice, becoming increasingly specialized and rigid only in the later years of secondary school.[45]

Inglis devoted his final chapter to matters of secondary school organization that transcended the curriculum issues he discussed in the previous chapter. After reviewing the issue of grade organization, Inglis endorsed the "three-three plan" for the secondary level—three years of junior high school followed by three years of senior high school. He reiterated the imperative for continual and gradual transition through the grades. Inglis summarized at length the arguments for and against specialized and comprehensive high schools and reached the following conclusion:

> On the whole it appears: (a) that special-type junior high schools are unjustifiable; (b) that special-type four-grade high schools or senior high schools are practicable in a very few large cities only; (c) that the comprehensive or composite or consolidated high school should be the standard type even in the largest cities.[46]

Inglis maintained that the desirability of conducting vocational education under the auspices of the school was an important consideration in favoring the comprehensive school. He warned, "The high school undertakes a great responsibility when it entrusts an important part of the pupils' education to commercial enterprises. Education must not be exploited by industry."[47]

Inglis closed the chapter with a brief discussion of instructional concerns that transcended the formal subject curriculum and that contributed to the aims and functions he held for secondary education. He recapitulated the pedagogical necessity of choosing subject matter based not on deference to the organized disciplines, but based instead upon a consideration of the nature of the learner and of the society. He advocated an instructional method he called "supervised teaching" that combined traditional lecture and recitation with opportunities for students to learn how to study. Inglis touted the only recently, and incompletely, recognized "peculiar educational possibilities of extra-curriculum activities and the necessity of welding the formal and informal activities of school life into a system of integrated education." Such an approach would take "an advance step" in "coordinating and unifying the experiences of the educand and in breaking down the barriers between the school and life."[48] Inglis called for a new conception of guidance "designed to permit the pupil to explore, try out, and thus gain some understanding of his own capacities, aptitudes, and interests," to expose the student to "opportunities of life and of education," and to familiarize the student "with the privileges, demands, and responsibilities of life in its various phases, vocational and avocational, social, civic, and moral."[49] Finally, Inglis exhorted the educative power of the social organization of daily school life:

> Socially conscious and socially cooperating American citizens cannot be developed through the school unless in the school those citizens are trained through actual participation in the cooperative activities of the school. Self-governing citizens can be developed only through some degree of exercise in actual self-government. The secondary school cannot and should not avoid its responsibility in this important form of education.[50]

Inglis advocated that participatory forms of student government should be a standard component of schooling from the elementary grades through the secondary school.

Principles of Secondary Education represented the first comprehensive review, evaluation, and synthesis of contemporary research, theory, and practice in secondary education. Inglis's method enabled him to make subtle but insightful contributions to the theory of secondary education that were at once rooted in tradition, consistent with the best available knowledge, responsive to contemporary social realities, and commensurate with ideals of democracy. *Principles* was more about the high school curriculum than about methods of instruction. Aspects of *Principles* almost amount to a repudiation of educational and professional commitments Inglis held earlier in his career. Inglis's early dedication to the teaching of Latin is conspicuous by its absence from his 1918 work. Here Inglis rejected the theory of "general discipline" upon which Latin was often justified and admitted only the most generic "direct value" for the study of Latin or any other foreign language, direct value that could be derived from the systematic study of any subject. Inglis found the recommendations of the Committee of Ten, which best characterized the kinds of curriculum he experienced as a student and then as a school teacher, highly problematic educationally and ill-suited to the needs of future citizens and of American society during the second decade of the twentieth century. Inglis had indeed come a long way since he left Wesleyan as a Latin scholar, both professionally and intellectually.

Inglis was in South Dakota participating in a survey of the state's educational system when, in late January 1918, his six author's copies of *Principles* arrived in Cambridge. During the next several months, Inglis requested that his publisher forward complimentary copies of *Principles* to numerous educational leaders, among them George D. Strayer, William H. Kilpatrick, Thomas H. Briggs, Clarence Kingsley, and his former teacher David Snedden.[51] Accolades for the book soon arrived at both Inglis's and Houghton Mifflin's offices. Ellwood Cubberley wrote, for example, that the book "sets a new mark in the subject, and that it ought to become the standard book in the subject in the colleges of the country." Referring to Houghton Mifflin's Riverside Textbooks in Education, which he edited, Cubberley continued, "It is a strong piece of work, and a fine addition to the series. A few big books like that, intended as substantial texts for college use, add dignity and give standing to the series."[52]

Within months of its publication, *Principles of Secondary Education* was favorably reviewed in *The School Review* and *The Nation*. Writing for the former journal, a reviewer judged that "Professor Inglis's book is the only worthy example" of a sole-authored text on secondary education. Pointing to Inglis's comprehensive consideration of extant research on every issue under discussion, the reviewer concluded that *Principles* was not only "more valuable and scientific than Snedden's book" on the secondary school, but that it was "the most scientific work on secondary education that has appeared in recent years."[53] The reviewer for *The Nation* praised Inglis's "industry. . . in culling from theoretical treatises the consensus of prevailing educational thought, and in substantiating his arguments by [presenting] a great series of tabulations and graphs." The reviewer criticized some of Inglis's terminology (e.g., "social-civic, economic-vocational, individualistic-avocational aims") as "unduly ponderous" and "redolent of academic convention," but regarded *Principles* as "a work admirable in scope" and otherwise "couched in clear language."[54]

Sales records for *Principles* are incomplete, but provide sufficient information to indicate that the work sold relatively well at the time for an academic textbook. These records can also provide a crude gauge of Inglis's influence, particularly when compared with other works. Houghton Mifflin's Riverside Textbooks in Education series featured the work of leading education professors in the United States. David

TABLE 3.1. Comparison of Book Sales Figures

	1917	1918	1919	1920	1921	1922	Total
Cubberly	2822	1576	2586	3111	3980	5382	19,457
Snedden	1773	476	437	757	194	398	4,035
Inglis	0	2012	3189	3406	2711	6325	17,643

Source: "Record of Book Sales, 1905–1923," MS Am 2030(33), Houghton Mifflin Papers, Houghton Library, Harvard University. *By permission of the Houghton Library, Harvard University.*

Snedden, Louis Terman, and Elwood Cubberley, general editor of the series, were among the high-profile authors in the Houghton Mifflin house. Table 3.1 compares sales figures (of number of books sold) for Cubberley's *Public School Administration*, Snedden's *Problems of Secondary Education* (1917), and Inglis's *Principles.*[55]

The comparison with Cubberley is significant because of his renown and influence in education at the time. That Inglis's sales closely approached Cubberley's perhaps indicates the degree of status that Inglis enjoyed in his day. The comparison with Snedden is more significant because both authors targeted the same audience: students of secondary education. After the publication of Inglis's book, sales of Snedden's text plummeted. Snedden advocated the separation of vocational and academic programs and pupils into distinct schools; Inglis embraced the unified comprehensive high school. The preference for Inglis's work over Snedden's reflected in these sales figures perhaps suggests that current historical interpretations exaggerate Snedden's influence on and representativeness of early twentieth-century thinking about secondary education.[56]

The shifts in Inglis's perspective on secondary education that began during his doctoral studies at Teachers College, Columbia University, resulted in "large consequences" that were evident by 1912 in his acceptance of a faculty appointment as professor of education at Rutgers College, in 1914 in his education scholarship, and were wrought most fully in his 1918 book, *Principles of Secondary Education.* In "the tome," as he called it, Inglis expressly repudiated traditional academic commitments manifest in the recommendations of the Committee of Ten, which had been emblematic of his experience as a high school and college student and as a high school teacher. During the period 1914–18, Inglis systematically analyzed extant theory and research about secondary education and constructed a masterful synthesis in *Principles.* In the process, rather than validating the cherished beliefs that guided the first ten years of his career, as the status politics thesis would predict, Inglis in fact invalidated those beliefs, transforming his theoretical perspective from the academic traditionalist position to the outlook of a progressive experimentalist.

Indeed, it is fair to say that *Principles of Secondary Education* manifests the "distinctive method of progressive reform" that has been reconstructed through decades of historical study of the period: thoroughly investigate a social problem, collect pertinent evidence, apply the modes of inquiry of the emerging social sciences to analyze that evidence, generate solutions that logically follow, work to implement the solution through a voluntary association.[57] Inglis's faith in the utility of new social sciences, another hallmark of progressivism, is particularly pronounced; from this perspective, *Principles of Secondary Education* stands as a quintessential statement of progressive values, as an attempt to generate organizing principles upon which to construct a new, responsive social institution.[58] Additionally, when the practical recommendations in *Principles* are viewed as a logical sequel to the conclusions in his dissertation, *The Rise of the High School in Massachusetts,* Inglis's work can be understood as a manifestation of the method of progressive historians, which sought "both to provide an account of how we came to the present moment of transition" and "to connect this account to a program for future action."[59] The transformation in Inglis's thinking about secondary education, completed in *Principles*, reflects the "revolution in secondary education" that Cremin discerned in the developments between 1893 and 1918.[60] Moreover, *Principles* represents an application to education of hallmarks of American pragmatism: commitment to the method of science, to democracy, and to the reconstruction of traditional patterns of action in response to changing social realities.[61] *Principles*, however, was just the beginning for Inglis. Over the next half dozen years he would participate in and contribute to some of the definitive aspects of the progressive education movement.

CHAPTER FOUR

Education Commissioner

Inglis participated in and contributed to the development of another quintessential expression of progressivism in education, the report of the Commission on the Reorganization of Secondary Education (CRSE), titled, *Cardinal Principles of Secondary Education*. For Cremin, the *Cardinal Principles* report represented the culmination of the "revolution" in secondary education in the United States that occurred since the 1893 Committee of Ten report. Like Inglis's 1918 book, the *Cardinal Principles* report manifests the progressive era impulse to generate organizing principles upon which to construct a responsive social institution. Although because of an eighteen-month gap in surviving archival records, the exact extent of Inglis's, or any CRSE member's influence on the report remains an open question, the preparation of the report clearly was a collaborative effort. The resemblance of the ideas advocated by Inglis in *Principles of Secondary Education* and by the CRSE in the *Cardinal Principles* report, however, appears indisputable. Inglis's participation in the development of the *Cardinal Principles* report, as well as his other professional activities during the period 1916–18, which included his service to the War Department's Committee on Education and Special Training, signal his transformation from academic traditionalist to progressive experimentalist.

Inglis and the *Cardinal Principles* Report

In 1913, the National Education Association's (NEA) Committee of Nine on the Articulation of High School and College, in a move reflecting the changing orientation of the committee's work, changed its name to the Commission on the Reorganization of Secondary Education. Comprised of a general reviewing committee and separate subject area committees, the CRSE sought to formulate recommendations for secondary education that responded to recent changes in the nature of society, in the secondary school population, and in educational theory, and that viewed the high school as something more than a downward extension of and ultimate preparation for the college. In January 1915, the general reviewing committee, led by the commission chair, Clarence Kingsley, began work on an overarching rationale for secondary education.[1]

Edward Krug's reconstruction of the activities of the CRSE and interpretation of the *Cardinal Principles* report long dominated historical scholarship. Krug argued that CRSE Chair Clarence Kingsley was the principal, if not the sole, author of the *Cardinal Principles* report and that, likely influenced by David Snedden, Kingsley was largely responsible for the social efficiency slant of the report. Krug implied that other CRSE members essentially acquiesced to Kingsley's views. Krug based his argument on similarities between proposals in Kingsley's earlier publications and proposals in the *Cardinal Principles* report and on an examination of archival documents. Krug characterized the vision of society presented in the report as "democracy as the age of social efficiency saw it."[2] Krug's contention that the report manifested social efficiency–social control ideology pivoted on the association of the *Cardinal Principles* report with Snedden through Kingsley.[3]

A reexamination of archival materials, combined with a consideration of pre-CRSE writings of other CRSE members, however, reveals substantive problems with Krug's account.[4] Because at least eight members of the CRSE's reviewing committee had, like Kingsley, previously advocated ideas that subsequently appeared in the 1918 report, often prior to their membership on the commission, these ideas cannot be attributed exclusively to Kingsley. A reexamination of the surviving records of the CRSE, moreover, reveals that while Krug's depiction of Kingsley's efficient administrative leadership is accurate, Krug's contention that Kingsley served as the intellectual author of the report is problematic. Archival records indicate that, in fact, reviewing committee members enjoyed regular input to drafts of the *Cardinal Principles* report, as they did to all other reports prepared under the auspices of the CRSE, that the reviewing committee actually voted on revisions, that revisions to Kingsley's section drafts were recommended by reviewing committee members, that Kingsley incorporated such changes into subsequent drafts, and that other CRSE members drafted other sections of the report. In short, contrary to the prevailing interpretation, available evidence indicates that the *Cardinal Principles* report was the product not of the lone work of the commission chair, but of the collaborative efforts of the entire commission.

Inglis came to the CRSE about a year after the reviewing committee had begun its work. The reviewing committee consisted of the chairs of sixteen subcommittees and ten members at large. On 24 February 1916, Inglis telegrammed Holmes, informing him of U.S. Commissioner of Education P. P. Claxton's desire that he serve on a "commission [on] university relations," a phrase that likely was shorthand for the previous name of the CRSE. According to the minutes of the CRSE meeting held in Detroit on 20, 21, and 22 February 1916, Inglis was in attendance and was assigned to review reports on ancient languages and foreign languages. Kingsley also appointed Inglis to a "committee to co-operate with him in revision the statement of the Commission."[5] The Committee on Ancient Languages and Foreign languages ultimately was unable to achieve consensus and never released a report, although Inglis was optimistic enough that it would to print an excerpt from an early draft in *Principles of Secondary Education.*[6] The special committee to which Kingsley added Inglis had been appointed at the February 1916 meeting by the reviewing committee to assist Kingsley with the revisions of the sections of the report for which he was responsible.[7] To what extent did Inglis contribute to the *Cardinal Principles* report?

Although archival records clearly indicate that the *Cardinal Principles* report represented the work of the collaboration of commission members, it was not unusual for individual members to assume responsibility for drafting sections of the report. For example, in a "Preliminary Plan" for the commissions work, Chairman Kingsley assigned himself the responsibility of drafting three proposed sections of the report, and assigned to nine other commission members the responsibility for drafting seven other sections.[8] Moreover, the CRSE archives contain drafts of sections prepared by individual commission members as well as evidence that the input of members was reflected in later drafts of the report. It is clear, for example, that Henry Neumann served as the principal author of the sections of the report that pertained to ethical values.[9] The limitations of the archival holdings, however, prevent a fuller accounting of the influence of individual commission members. Records of the CRSE between June 1916 and the publication of the *Cardinal Principles* report in 1918 unfortunately contain documents relating only to a schedule of its publication and plans to disseminate the report nationally. The numerous section drafts, correspondence, minutes, and action lists that characterize the records for the first eighteen months of the commission's work simply do not exist for the last eighteen months of the commission's endeavors. Surviving CRSE records provide no clue as to the deliberations about the substance and wording of the report during the eighteen months immediately preceding its publication. A search for personal papers of CRSE members yielded no substantive documents pertaining to the commission's work during that period.

This gap in archival materials is unfortunate because the commission prepared most of the *Cardinal Principles* report during the last eighteen months before its publication. A comparison of the last unpublished draft of the report, dated June 1916, and the published report is instructive. The 1916 draft was less than half the length of the 1918 report. Of the eight sections of the 1916 draft, six appeared in the 1918 report in revised and expanded form, one appeared nearly verbatim, and portions of one were incorporated into another. In the 1916 draft Kingsley indicated that two sections, vocational guidance and organization of differentiated curriculums, were still under preparation by other reviewing committee members. With the 1916 draft Kingsley also queried steering committee members, "What other topics should be added?"[10] Of the nineteen sections that appeared in the 1918 report, eight had not appeared in the 1916 draft. These eight sections amounted to fourteen and a half pages of the total twenty-five pages of text in the published 1918 report. All of the material on the secondary curriculum and on the comprehensive high school appeared in these last eight sections. In these eight sections of the *Cardinal Principles* report the CRSE articulated the specializing and unifying functions of secondary education, characterizing them as "supplementary." Here the commission organized the curriculum into "constants," "variables," and "free electives." Here the commission regarded vocational guidance as critical to achieving the specializing function and school activities as crucial in achieving the unifying function. Here the commission proposed that academic and vocational education be housed under the same roof. Here the commission resoundingly endorsed the comprehensive high school as "the standard type of secondary school in the United States."[11]

The gap also corresponds with eighteen of the twenty-four months during which Inglis served on the CRSE. Inglis's input to the report, however, can be gauged in other ways. A comparison of Kingsley's 1915 "Topics Suggested for Treatment in the Report of the Reviewing Committee" and the 1916 "Draft of Report of Reviewing Committee of the Commission on Secondary Education Appointed by the National Education Association" with the published *Cardinal Principles* report (1918) is revealing in this regard. In this comparison, it is apparent that many of the principles Inglis advanced in his 1918 book and in his earlier writings appear in the *Cardinal Principles* report, but not in the two earlier documents. Inglis had no input to the 1915 document and only last minute access to the 1916 document as a new member of the reviewing committee. Although this evidence is little more than circumstantial, the fact that the ideas that most resembled Inglis's were introduced to the *Cardinal Principles* report after he joined the reviewing committee strengthens the case for his influence. Of course, other members of the reviewing committee, such as Charles Hughes Johnston of the University of Illinois and Frank M. Leavitt of the Pittsburgh public schools who were assigned later sections of the report, likely influenced the final document, as well.

Of all of the CRSE members, however, it was Inglis whose views most closely and thoroughly parallel the conception of secondary education articulated in the *Cardinal Principles* report. As discussed earlier, in an article published in the May 1915 issue of *Teachers College Record*, Inglis articulated the core principles of his theory of secondary education that subsequently he would elaborate in his 1918 book.[12] Inglis held that a "certain degree of unity in feeling, in habit, in ideas, in conduct, in thought is a necessity of any form of society." This necessity "is greater in a democracy than in any other form of society."[13] Inglis suggested that the increasing diversity of American society and the corresponding need for unity held the greatest implications for the social-civic and individualistic-avocational aims of secondary education. He proposed that two phases, or functions, of secondary education must be provided through the educational program of the school in order that both of these aims are met: "integration" and "differentiation." He emphasized that to oppose integration and differentiation against each other was "fallacious" and that they were in fact "supplementary." Inglis claimed that "integration and differentiation must be conceived not as conflicting with each other but as supplementary phases of the same unitary process."[14] In strikingly similar language, the CRSE stated, "The ideal of democracy . . . involves . . . unification whereby the members of that democracy may obtain those common ideas, common ideals, and common modes of thought, feeling, and action that make for cooperation, social cohesion, and social solidarity."[15] The differentiation and integration functions that served by 1915 as the cornerstone of Inglis's theory of secondary education appeared in the *Cardinal Principles* report as the "supplementary" specializing and unifying functions of the comprehensive high school.[16]

In fact, the extent to which Inglis's 1918 *Principles of Secondary Education* and the CRSE's *Cardinal Principles* report overlap is considerable, as Simmons observed.[17] Simmons documented the advocacy of the following concepts in both the *Cardinal Principles* report and Inglis's *Principles of Secondary Education*: "continuous growth concept; individual differences; endorsement of the junior high school idea; social purposes of education; endorsement of vocational education; high school not exclusively college preparatory in function; stress subjects' direct values; opposition of 'logical organization' of subject matter; secondary school subjects should meet the needs of students."[18] Additional points of congruence include rejection of mental discipline, advocacy of the criterion of utility in selecting subject matter, embracement of wide range of education aims, organization of the curriculum into constants and variables, endorsement of the three–three organization of secondary education, promotion of a democratic approach to school administration, and resounding endorsement of the comprehensive high school. Inglis unequivocally concluded: "the comprehensive or composite or consolidated high school should be the standard type even in the largest cities."[19] The CRSE similarly concluded: "The comprehensive (sometimes called composite or cosmopolitan) high school, embracing all curriculums in one unified organization, should remain the standard type of secondary education in the United States."[20] The parallels between Inglis's work and the *Cardinal Principles* report are clear.

The direction of the influence, however, represents another historical question. After summarizing the similarities between Inglis's book and the *Cardinal Principles* report, Simmons suggested, "Whether Inglis borrowed these ideas from the Commission, gave them to the Commission, or formulated them simultaneously with but independently of the Commission is inconsequential. The fact remains that, through his book, these principles gained wide circulation among professional educators and teachers-in-training."[21] Inglis, in fact, as noted had published an article in May 1915 in *Teachers College Record*, prior to his membership on the CRSE, that expressed ideas that appeared in the *Cardinal Principles* report and had begun work on his book by the fall of 1915. He joined the CRSE in February 1916. By December 1916 Inglis was making final revisions to his lengthy manuscript based upon feedback he had solicited from "specialists" in secondary education; he submitted the revised manuscript to Houghton Mifflin in July 1917, completed proofs of graphs in September 1917, submitted figures and graphs in October 1917, and checked page proofs in November 1917. His six author's copies arrived in Cambridge in January 1918. Kingsley forwarded the final draft of the *Cardinal Principles* report to the CRSE reviewing committee in June 1917, which was scheduled to go to the printer after 1 September 1917, and which was published during early 1918. Although the possibility of the CRSE influencing Inglis cannot be ruled out, the fact that he had published his basic ideas and had begun work on his manuscript prior to his joining the CRSE and had already by fall 1916 sent drafts of a manuscript that would come in at 722 pages when published for review, suggest that much, if not most, of his work was completed before his CRSE membership. Indeed, the exhaustive review of theory and research that undergirds Inglis's conclusions and recommendations is too elaborate to have originated at the eleventh hour. Moreover, the fact that the ideas that resembled ideas in his book appeared in the *Cardinal Principles* report only after he was a member, suggests that influence likely flowed from Inglis to the commission. In any event, much of the thinking about the secondary school that appeared in both Inglis's book and the CRSE's report was circulating in educational discussions of the day. Unless additional documentary sources emerge, the matter of the direction of influence cannot be settled definitively.

Inglis's influence on the report, however, may also be indirectly gauged by the impressions of his contemporaries. William H. Kilpatrick, a member of the commission's special reviewing committee with Inglis, recorded in his diary that Inglis attended the 26 February 1917 meeting of the commission and characterized him as one of the "better men" on the reviewing committee, which, by itself, though complimentary, tells us little except perhaps that Inglis participated actively in the commission's deliberations.[22] Inglis's colleagues at Harvard were confident about his contributions to the report. At the memorial service conducted by the Harvard Graduate School of Education after Inglis's sudden death at the age of forty-four in 1924, Dean Henry Wyman Holmes noted that Inglis "played a commanding part in the work of the Commission."[23] Colleague Frederick Edson Clerk claimed, "The work of the Commission was most thorough and comprehensive, and yet when it came to the Reviewing Committee, the searching scrutiny and unprejudiced analysis by Dr. Inglis and his associates frequently changed the original judgments and always improved them."[24] In another memorial, Holmes noted, "Professor Inglis did especially important work, contributing much to the chief publication of the Commission."[25] Additionally, L. Thomas Hopkins, Inglis's student, recalled in his memoir that Inglis "was somewhat incense[d] at the difficulty of convincing commission members that existing secondary education was as out-of-date as the rough tools of the caveman."[26] Hopkins was under the impression that Inglis had chaired the commission, suggesting that Hopkins recalled Inglis enjoying great influence over it. In summary, then, although additional documentation is necessary to arrive at a definitive explanation, indications are that Inglis likely contributed substantively to the *Cardinal Principles* report. That Inglis, as well as other CRSE members who clearly contributed to the report, did not embrace the extreme social efficiency-social control ideology that historians attribute to the report through indirect association with Snedden, provides good reason to interpret the work of the CRSE in a new light, one that casts the values of pedagogical progressives in sharper relief than the ideology of administrative progressives.[27]

Meanwhile, for Inglis, 1918 was a banner year. In addition to *Principles* and the *Cardinal Principles* report, three articles and one book review he had written were published that year. Inglis also assumed responsibilities as a member of the editorial board of *Educational Administration and Supervision*, a position he held until 1923; Charles Hughes Johnston, Inglis's colleague on the CRSE, founded the journal in 1915 at the University of Illinois.[28] Two of Inglis's 1918 articles appeared in *Educational Administration and Supervision*. All three extended principles he promulgated in his book and advocated through his work on the commission.

In a generally favorable review of Colvin's *An Introduction to High School Teaching* published in *School and Society*, Inglis suggested that Colvin could have devoted more attention to supervised study and, noting that Colvin's practical examples of classroom activities applied exclusively to academic subjects, called for additional attention to "practical arts instruction." In one of the few instances in which he wrote anything about classroom discipline, Inglis suggested that Colvin "might still more have stressed the importance of discipline as a positive means of education instead of as a means of control."[29]

In the discussion of the relation of secondary education to higher education he presented in *Principles*, Inglis had examined the advantages and disadvantages of standardized examinations, especially those used for college admission decisions. For Inglis, the disadvantages clearly outweighed the purported advantages. He noted, for example, that "single tests commonly do not indicate the true status of an individual with regard to any single mental trait" and insisted that the "true status of an individual in any mental trait is to be determined by a number of separate measures."[30] This imperative for compiling multiple indicators of student learning would by the 1930s become a basic principle of curriculum evaluation. Inglis had also criticized the tendency of high-stakes college entrance exams to reduce the secondary school curriculum to a matter of the student simply "securing . . . 'points' or 'credits'" toward graduation and to reduce instruction to the trivial task of "cramming." In the process, he argued, sustained academic study for the purpose of achieving "high standards of real attainment" were lost.[31] Little doubt Inglis drew here from his experience in the college prep environment of the Horace Mann School.

In a 1918 article for *Educational Administration and Supervision*, Inglis examined Thorndike's finding that the reliability of teachers' grading of student work was disappointingly low. Inglis presented his analysis of data pertaining to graders of College Entrance Examination Board (CEEB) tests. He found that the variability among CEEB graders was lower than that of "teachers in general." Inglis concluded that although the CEEB gradings were "about as accurate as they can be made by fallible human judges," the "difficulty of determining merit on the basis of single examinations" remained.[32] In an article published in *School and Society* that year, Inglis examined the issue of grade distributions in college courses. Studying Harvard undergraduates, he compared grades received in elective courses to "standard" grade distributions typically employed by professors. Inglis found that student grades in such courses "conform more nearly to the distribution of grades formerly received than to the 'typical distribution.'"[33] He concluded that educators should consider the limitations of employing standard distributions in course grading. Both of these articles reflect Inglis's commitment to the new statistical or "scientific" study of education and his interest in suggesting implications of such research for educational practice.

In another article published in 1918 in *Educational Administration and Supervision*, Inglis argued that wartime conditions underscored the need to implement the proposals of the CRSE.[34] He examined the implications of American involvement in the Great War for the following dimensions of secondary education: social-civic; economic-vocational; education for the worthy use of leisure; moral education; physical education; subject matter; and the organization and administration of secondary education. With respect to social-civic education, for example, Inglis explicitly endorsed the recommendations of the CRSE's Committee on Social Studies for the "Community Civics" curriculum and the "Problems of Democracy" course as appropriate vehicles for enacting democratic ideals.[35] Inglis also called for "more adequate provision for economic-vocational education" but also warned that in some cases this priority was "so exaggerated as to over-emphasize that phase of education to the minimizing or neglect of other necessary phases of education." In this regard, he characterized the Smith-Hughes Act as "pernicious."[36] In short, Inglis insisted on a balanced secondary curriculum that stressed no single "phase" at the expense of others, thus serving all students equitably.

In this article Inglis commented on other contemporary educational issues as well. On the matter of military training in high schools, Inglis did "not favor the requirement of military training for boys in the secondary school, unless the same or equivalent requirement is made for boys outside the secondary school."[37] Inglis dismissed arguments that subjects such as science and foreign languages should garner curricular priority due to exigencies of the conflict. He reasoned, as he had in *Principles*, that the value of a study should be determined by its direct utility to the pupil. He also condemned the "hysterical outcry against the study of German" instigated by wartime propaganda.[38] In short, Inglis maintained that although wartime conditions created no new principles of secondary education, they did reaffirm the need to consider reasonably the function and nature of secondary education with an eye toward the kind of reorganization proposed in the *Cardinal Principles* report. Before the year was out, Inglis would enjoy the opportunity to contribute directly to the educational phase of the war effort.

Committee on Education and Special Training

The entry in 1917 of the United States into the Great War precipitated widespread mobilization for the military effort. Within a year after Congress' 6 April 1917 declaration of war on Germany, Secretary of War Newton D. Baker appointed the Committee on Education and Special Training (CEST) "for the purpose of organizing and coordinating all of the educational resources of the country with relation to the needs of the Army."[39] General Order No. 15, dated February 1918, identified the following functions of the CEST:

> To study the needs of the various branches of the service for skilled men and technicians; to determine how such needs shall be met, whether by selective draft, special training in educational institutions or otherwise; to secure the cooperation of the educational institutions of the country and to represent the War Department in its relations with such institutions; to administer such a plan of special training in colleges and schools as may be adopted.[40]

Beginning in the spring of 1918, shortly after the first American troops disembarked on the Continent, the CEST coordinated the training of military recruits "in the simple underlying operations of carpentry, metalworking, blacksmithing, auto management and other mechanical activities useful in the army" through existing educational institutions around the country.[41]

In mid-October 1918, Harvard President Lowell agreed with a War Department request that Inglis replace Holmes in his responsibilities at the CEST.[42] Although the exact nature of Holmes' and Inglis's duties on the CEST is unclear, Inglis likely concerned himself with phasing out the CEST activities.[43] The Great War ended two weeks after Inglis arrived in Washington under a leave of absence from Harvard that extended to the new year. Although subsequently identified as a significant phase of his career, Inglis's services to the CEST were likely administrative in nature and unrelated substantively to his professional commitments in the area of secondary education. Inglis did not return to Cambridge for the spring 1919 semester as had been expected. In December 1918, the Virginia Public Schools Education Commission, which during the previous spring had been established in a bill passed by the state assembly of Virginia, invited Inglis to direct a comprehensive survey of public schooling in the state.[44] His leave of absence extended to 1 June 1919, Inglis established residence in Richmond to direct the survey. Antoinette, who had remained in Cambridge during Inglis's two months in Washington, DC, joined Alexander in the Virginia capitol.

Inglis's work on the CRSE and his 1918 publications further manifested his commitment to principles of progressive education that he had begun to articulate during his tenure at Rutgers College and which he systematically elaborated in *Principles of Secondary Education*. By 1918, if not earlier, Inglis's transformation from a Latinist with traditional academic loyalties to a progressive experimentalist was complete. As he did on the CRSE, for the next six years, Inglis would continue to advocate these principles and would apply them to various aspects of secondary education.

CHAPTER FIVE

School Surveyor

Inglis's survey work provides additional indication of his advocacy of principles of progressive education as well as an opportunity to test accepted interpretations of the survey movement against previously untapped documentation. Although historians have considered the school survey movement in the context either of broad historical treatments of the period or of specialized historical studies, the task of reconstructing a systematic history of the movement itself remains. Just one of the Inglis surveys is cited in existing historical treatments of the movement. During his career, Inglis participated in nine school surveys. He served as a staffer on surveys of the states of Washington, South Dakota, and Indiana, and directed surveys in Westchester, NY, Winchester, VA, Augusta, ME, Swansea, MA, and the state of Virginia. In his least direct role on a survey, Inglis served on the reviewing committee for a survey of the Baltimore schools. Although the extent to which these nine surveys are representative of the hundreds conducted at that time is unclear, they do represent at least as much as if not more data than that upon which historians seem, to date, to have based their interpretations. The following discussion of Inglis's survey work is organized around three major aspects of the survey movement recognized in current interpretations. A historiographical discussion of the survey movement precedes an analysis of Inglis's survey work.

As noted earlier, between roughly 1910 and 1930, professors of education conducted over six hundred surveys of state, city, county, and municipal school systems across the country. A survey could target a particular problem that a school system faced, or could involve an exhaustive investigation of an entire system. Historians generally have depicted the survey movement as a manifestation of a contemporary commitment to the promotion of social efficiency-social control doctrine. Historians have also characterized the survey movement as an effort to impose business values on the public schools. When discussing the survey movement, however, educational and curriculum historians have cited on average only two to three surveys in support of their interpretation.

Historical perspectives on the survey movement are reasonably categorized in terms of histories written prior to 1960 and those written after 1960. Historical studies written during this first period tended to emphasize the role of the survey movement in bringing a greater respect for evidence to problem solving and decision making about educational matters. Caswell, for example, highlighted the survey's "scientific spirit" and emphasized the survey's contribution to "the movement which is basing human thought and conduct on facts objectively measured, rather than on the assertion of authority."[1] For Caswell, the school survey essentially represented an improved use of evidence in educational decision making. Knight also stressed the significance of the "scientific" nature of surveys, concluding, "The survey movement has helped to change school administration from a business of guesswork to one that is at least approximately scientific in theory if not always so in actual practice."[2] Similarly, Edwards and Richey noted the reliance on expert opinion during the early years of the movement, from about 1911 to 1914, and the advent of scientific appraisals beginning around 1915, and suggested that surveys contributed to the "developing science of education."[3]

Historical studies prepared after 1960 typically emphasized the role of the survey movement in propagating business values and in promoting social efficiency and social control. Callahan, for example, observed that the "growth in numbers [in the hundreds] of the surveys paralleled the growth of the strength of the efficiency movement and the accompanying criticism of the schools in the years after 1911."[4] Although Callahan noted that "the dominant motivating force in most instances was economic, not educational," he also acknowledged that "the outlooks and competence of the surveyors influenced the nature of the survey."[5] Callahan allowed for distinguishing nuances in the work of those educators who rallied beneath the banner of "efficiency." According to Krug, surveys were a way "to move this alleged mass of foot draggers [principals and teachers] in the desired directions," that is, toward the "acceptance of the doctrines" of scientific management and social efficiency.[6] Similarly, Tyack claimed that the "school survey became a favorite technique to spread the program of the administrative progressives."[7] He characterized administrative progressives as preoccupied with "organizational behavior and the linkage of school and external control, with aggregate goals rather than individual development of students." Working within the educational system as quintessential "insiders," administrative progressives "focused upon differentiating the structure and fulfilling the goals of social efficiency and control."[8] Lagemann, whose work represents an exception to this trend, examined the role of surveys in the history of educational research. The "accumulation of 'school facts'" would create a "science" of education that could help explain school practice. She suggested that the survey movement contributed to the rise of "experts" in education and characterized the survey method as a "quintessentially 'progressive' technology."[9]

Because of the recent dominance of the social efficiency–social control interpretation of the survey movement, this chapter evaluates the extent to which significant dimensions of "social efficiency" are manifest in the Inglis surveys. Specifically, economic dimensions (i.e., cost effectiveness), organizational dimensions (e.g., imposition of external control through, among other things, aggregate goals), and educational dimensions (e.g., curriculum content and differentiation, classroom instruction) are discussed. The extent to which the Inglis surveys are explainable through the prevailing social efficiency thesis is assessed, and aspects of the Inglis surveys that appear anomalous to the social efficiency-control thesis are discussed.

The Inglis Surveys

In his survey work, Inglis collaborated with some of the most influential educators of the day, among them Paul Hanus and Walter Dearborn, both his colleagues at Harvard, and P. P. Claxton, U.S. Commissioner of Education, as well as educators Thomas Jesse Jones, Ellwood Cubberley, and Abraham Flexner, and psychologists Louis Terman and Robert Yerkes. Attributing specific recommendations in these survey reports to Inglis or any participating individual is sometimes problematic. Members of survey teams may have drafted the chapter of the report to which they contributed, or may have simply submitted a subreport from which the survey director generated the final report. Or, the chapter may appear in the final report largely as they prepared it. On the one hand, for example, archival records and remarks by a fellow surveyor at Inglis's Harvard memorial service indicate that he contributed substantively to the Washington and Virginia surveys.[10] On the other hand, the case of the Baltimore survey is particularly difficult; Inglis served on a six-member reviewing committee that examined the reports of the survey commission. He was directly responsible for no aspect of the survey proper; his name appeared, with those of his five fellow reviewing committee members, at the end of a two and a half page statement that accompanied the three-volume, 1,072-page report. Thus, attributing any recommendation of either the Baltimore Survey Commission or its reviewing committee to Inglis, or to any committee member, is virtually impossible.[11] Notwithstanding these limitations of the evidence at hand, an examination of the economic, organizational, and educational dimensions of the aspects of the surveys for which Inglis was identified as having responsibility can shed light both on Inglis's career and on historical interpretations of the survey movement.

Economic Dimensions

The economic dimensions of the social efficiency–social control thesis refer to the extent to which Inglis's survey work manifests Tayloristic principles of scientific management that conceive of efficiency in terms of economy and cost cutting. Again, in his discussion of the survey movement, Callahan claimed that "the dominant motivating force was economic, not educational. What was wanted was a decrease or at least no increase in taxes," Callahan continued. Economic concerns, of course, are reasonable priorities, especially during a period of time when enrollments were expanding rapidly, often so rapidly that school systems could not keep pace with demands for additional resources. Callahan's concern was that, too frequently, economic concerns trumped educational needs.[12]

As discussed earlier, the survey Inglis conducted in Westchester County, New York, in 1912 represented an effort on the part of school officials "to co-operate with the general movement . . . for increasing the efficiency of our immense and costly system of public schools."[13] Recall that, after compiling the requisite statistical information and even generating efficiency indexes, Inglis concluded his report by appealing to officials and citizens in Westchester County to embrace a wider definition of efficiency:

> There are several ways of promoting economy and efficiency. One is by saving money; another is by obtaining more or better service, or both, for the same money; a third is by increasing both the quality and quantity of service up to the full standard of service demanded by the citizen, even though the expenditure is therefore increased.
>
> To obtain less or poorer service than is paid for, to obtain less or poorer service than is needed, is waste.[14]

Inglis advanced a conception of efficiency that went beyond conventional concerns about cost effectiveness. For Inglis, educational efficiency was a matter of providing students with the education they needed, regardless of cost.

In the surveys of the state educational systems of Washington (1916) and South Dakota (1918), Inglis shared with S. P. Capen and Harold W. Foght, both of the U.S. Bureau of Education, responsibility for analyzing institutions of higher education. Both survey reports identified unnecessary duplication of programs in higher education institutions and recommended reorganizations that would consolidate redundant programs into a smaller number of institutions and called for greater articulation between secondary and higher education.[15] The South Dakota survey included the recommendation to remove college preparatory programs, "preparatory departments" as they were called, from higher education institutions and to locate them in public high schools.[16] Clearly, cost effectiveness underlies concern for duplication of programs in various branches of the system and potentially smacks of an economic conception of "efficiency."

Yet these surveyors were not wedded to Tayloristic iterations of educational efficiency. Their fundamental commitment was in providing the best education the tax dollar could buy. In some cases, such as in the elimination of redundant programs, reduction of unnecessary expenditures was a logical concern. In other cases, education efficiency meant an increase in expenditures. Inglis, Capen, and Foght, for example, noted that with "relatively few exceptions the salaries paid to faculty members in the State university, the State college, and the State school of mines are low—so low that the efficiency of instruction is seriously imperiled."[17] Here, efficiency connoted quality. A subsequent recommendation called for spending sufficient funds to secure effective teachers. Additionally, they identified low "salary cost per clock hour" as an indication of poor educational decision making and rather than lauding such behavior as a wise, frugal use of funds, they recommended that "the administrative officers of the institutions should determine whether the excessively low cost is due (a) to teaching programs which are excessively heavy, (b) overlarge classes, (c) excessively low salaries."[18] In fact, they found that expenditures at South Dakota State University were lower than those of comparable institutions in other states. They concluded: "It is therefore possible to incur additional expense of about $ 20,000 annually for the needs of the university, whether it be for increased salaries . . . or for other purposes, without going beyond the suggested standard."[19] For Inglis, Capen, and Foght, educational efficiency, stated in financial terms, meant not conducting a program as cheaply as possible, but rather spending sufficient sums to provide effective educational services. Efficiency was as much a matter of quality and efficacy, as it was of economy. This position echoes Inglis's recommendation to the Westchester County school authorities in 1912.

Inglis's 1919 survey of the educational system of the state of Virginia also recommended increasing expenditure on education programs, especially those that served African American students. Acknowledgment of the disparity between educational conditions for blacks and whites pervaded the Virginia report, not only as represented in statistical data, but also as documented graphically in photographs that appeared throughout.[20] The survey staff recommended improvements to virtually every aspect of the education of African American students, from the training and compensation of teachers, to the conditions and equipment of schools, to courses of study, to the improvement of roads so that African American children could travel to school. They recommended more supervisors to assist African American teachers than to assist white teachers. In the Virginia survey, increasing expenditures was the only acceptable alternative for improving education for all children in the Commonwealth.

The report of the survey of Swansea, Massachusetts, described five significant findings of the survey staff's work, three of which pertain to economic dimensions of social efficiency. First, only one of the ten elementary school buildings was considered "as offering satisfactory or adequate features."[21] Second, Swansea's per pupil expenditure was approximately twice the statewide average, due largely to the exorbitant cost of sending adolescents to nearby Fall River High School on a tuition basis. This expense also drained financial resources from the Swansea elementary school, which received a disproportionately small share of the annual budget. Third, a high turnover rate among teachers in Swansea schools was considered to have a negative impact on the education of the town's children. The survey team recommended the elimination of one room schools and the consolidation of elementary schools and the construction of a high school in the Swansea community as the only way "to provide the fullest range of educational opportunities for all the children of both elementary and secondary school age."[22] The implementation of these recommendations would, of course, accrue an additional financial burden, at least in the short run. As in other surveys in which Inglis had participated, the Swansea survey connected effectiveness with economy, but in terms of valuing both yet emphasizing the former. Spending more on the educational program could prove economically wise in the long run as long as a significant educational return was made on the investment and Swansea's money was better spent on its own system rather than transferred to local Fall River.

The report of the survey of the schools of Augusta, Maine, found finances in relatively good shape. Again, recommendations were characterized not by interest in cutting cost, but by concerns about underfunding. Recommendations included suggestions not only for the building program, but also for raising teacher salaries, adding positions such as assistant school nurse and head janitor, and adding a testing program.[23] While the survey staff judiciously cautioned, "[w]ith increase in costs there should go careful study at every point to economize without sacrificing efficiency," it clearly distinguished economy from efficiency—the former referring to financial concerns and the latter to educational efficacy.[24] Significantly, with respect to financial considerations, the survey concluded, "Good schools are the hope of our democracy. Good schools, however, cost money."[25] The survey staff expressed confidence in the people of Augusta "to provide the money necessary" for good schools. Most of the report was devoted to describing the features of "good schools."

In the Inglis surveys, then, a concern but not a preoccupation with economy is apparent. Contrary to Callahan's general conclusion, in the Inglis surveys, the emphasis typically fell not on accruing the lowest cost, but on "producing the finest product" that money could buy.[26] Economy was not an end in itself, but a means to improving quality and equality of educational opportunity. And in many instances, improving quality and equality of educational opportunities required the expenditure of additional funds.

Organizational Dimensions

The organizational dimensions of the social efficiency–social control thesis involve the imposition of a corporate model of governance on school systems, a model that relied upon professional expertise differentiated into specialized tasks within the bureaucratic structure. For Tyack, the agenda of the "administrative progressives" to centralize authority over urban education decision making to a small citywide board of directors represented an effort to deracinate local control of schools from wards and to place it in the hands of a social elite who exploited professional expertise, personified by the emerging class of superintendents, to conduct the business of schooling. This corporate model of schooling sought to maintain social control by fitting students into the existing social order and pursuing collective goals at the expense of promoting students' individual development.[27] To what extent does Inglis's survey work manifest the agenda of the administrative progressives?

Inglis's survey work involved only two instances in which his responsibilities included analysis of school governance. Although some of the tactics that Tyack associated with the agenda of the administrative progressives appear in Inglis's recommendations, they were neither consistently applied nor were their motives consistent with those Tyack detected behind that agenda. The Virginia survey team, for example, found that state law provided that the eight-member State Board of Education, six of whom were ex officio from other government posts and two of whom were appointed by the ex officio members, appointed all county, district, and city superintendents statewide. The state superintendent, one of the ex officio members of the state board, was popularly elected. The survey team maintained that these provisions unduly politicized educational authority in the state. The survey team recommended amendments to the state constitution and laws that would make the state board members appointed by the governor with Senate approval and the state superintendent appointed by the state board.

The Virginia survey team found that, in addition to the fact that city superintendents were appointed by the state board, city boards of education were selected by ward, with the result that board members tended to represent special interests rather than the educational interests of the entire city. The survey team recommended that, in order for board members to represent the interests of the entire city, they be popularly elected and that city boards appoint city superintendents. The survey team also recommended the drawing of sharp legal distinctions between the "legislative and judicial" functions of the boards and the "professional and managerial functions of school administration," the appropriate province of the superintendents. Additionally, the team recommended that superintendent appointees meet professional qualifications that included completion of some postsecondary education, possession of a state teaching certificate, and teaching experience.[28] In the Augusta survey, Inglis also indicated the preferability of "representation at large" rather than by ward, but in light of the fact that the Augusta board appeared to function admirably, did not recommend that a change be made to popular election of board members.[29]

Inglis's survey work includes other recommendations for consolidating and centralizing control in the education systems he examined. To address the evident lackluster performance of Virginia's rural students, Inglis's survey staff recommended ten improvements to the education system. These improvements included legislating compulsory attendance, lengthening the school year to at least 180 days, upgrading qualifications of teachers and increasing supervision of teachers, consolidating one-room school houses and limiting them to five grades.[30] The reviewing committee of the Baltimore survey recommended moving authority over schools from the mayor's office to the Board of School commissioners and the superintendent, which, in effect, represents a decentralization of authority.[31] In Swansea, the survey team proposed a four-phase plan to replace gradually the ten elementary schools and attendance at neighboring Fall River High School arrangement with three consolidated elementary schools and a new high school located in the Swansea community.[32]

Figure 5.1. Virginia School Survey. *Left to right*: Former Superintendent Effinger, Alexander Inglis, Superintendent Paxton, Rockbridge, VA, 1919. Log School House Built 1871. Courtesy of David M. Brooks. Collection of Author.

In several surveys, Inglis's commitment to a differentiated bureaucratic structure characterized by specialized roles is apparent. In Virginia, for example, he recommended increasing the number of supervisors for both white and African American schools.[33] In Indiana, Inglis addressed the need to secure enough qualified teachers to teach specialized subjects, to keep teaching loads at a reasonable level—no more than six classes per day per teacher—and to avoid the assignment of teachers to subjects for which they had no preparation. Additionally, he recommended that the state maintain a staff of "at least five high school inspectors, one for every 150 high schools . . . if state supervision is to mean more than an occasional call."[34] Inglis recommended for the elementary grades in Augusta "the employment of a supervisor whose entire time is devoted to the improvement of instruction in these grades by personal work with the teachers."[35] The reviewing committee of the Baltimore survey recommended that the superintendent "should have associated with him an adequate staff of competent administrative and supervisory officers directly responsible to him."[36] In the Inglis surveys, specialized bureaucratic roles were taken for granted as vehicles for improving the educational effectiveness of school systems.

Yet, for Inglis, consolidation, centralization, and differentiation did not come at the expense of local needs, but in response to them. In Virginia, for example, the survey staff recommended the reorganization of Virginia high schools for the short run into a 5–3–3 pattern, with the intention of moving to a 6–3–3 organization. The survey staff recommended, however, that given variations in enrollments around the state, statewide "standardization" was unrealistic, and recognized the necessity of adapting reorganization to local conditions and needs.[37] The Swansea plan would not only result in updated facilities, but it would also enable the system to develop a curriculum suited to its local needs and more effectively articulated across the grade levels. By establishing its own high school, the Swansea community would retain local control over secondary education, rather than continue to abrogate control to neighboring Fall River. The high school was envisioned as housing grades seven through twelve. Grades seven and eight were envisioned as providing a smoother transition from elementary to secondary school work than was possible in the existing fragmented system.[38] The reviewing committee of the Baltimore survey also called for local discretion in the implementation of some survey recommendations.[39] In these instances, centralization served local interests.

The Inglis surveys also recognized that centralization could stifle local needs. In Indiana, Inglis found the state requirements for subjects to be so extensive that schools with small faculties could not feasibly meet them. Inglis found that the "extended and complex high school courses required by law and recommended by the state board of education have rendered difficult an effective and economical organization of instruction." These requirements prompted "over-ambitious attempt[s] to offer a program of studies beyond the resources and needs of the [local] community."[40] Often, to meet staffing needs at the local high school, systems short-changed elementary schools; teachers also taught subjects for which they had no preparation. Inglis found that during the 1920–1 school year, while the average cost per pupil for all high schools was $ 123, of "225 high schools enrolling each not more than 50 pupils, 85 showed a cost per pupil enrolled of more than $ 150, and 22, a per pupil cost above $ 200."[41] He concluded: "The net results are inferior education for the children, overburdened teachers, and an unjustifiable drain on the financial resources of the community."[42] Inglis recommended reducing the breadth of high school offerings and employing a proportional and appropriate number of teachers. This would mean reducing the staff in high schools where programs exceeded community needs and increasing the staff in underresourced schools.

Aspects of the agenda of administrative progressives appear in Inglis's survey work, but not to the degree that historians have documented it in the survey work of other educators, such as Ellwood Cubberley or Jesse Sears. In the surveys in which Inglis recommended changes in governance of educational systems, notably for Virginia and Augusta, the stated aim was to depoliticize a system that demonstrably fostered political patronage at the expense of educational effectiveness. While Inglis accepted the centralized city school board, he sought to decentralize state control over education by transferring appointment of superintendents from the state board to local boards. Political patronage was also to be undermined by substitution of election of board members by popular vote for selection by ward. Additionally, Inglis stopped short of proposing such changes when the existing system seemed to work, as it did in Augusta. Moreover, when recommending such changes, Inglis appealed not to business ideology, but to political principle. Because Inglis generally seems to have taken "the hierarchical structure of differentiated schooling as a given" and instead focused on the educational aspects of the school systems he surveyed, he perhaps better manifested characteristics of the reformers Tyack dubbed "pedagogical progressives."[43] For Inglis, bureaucratic organization should function not at the expense of, but in the interest of, local control over and continued improvement of educational quality and opportunity.

Educational Dimensions

According to Tyack, pedagogical progressives "spoke about the 'project method,' the 'activity curriculum,' and other ways to 'meet individual needs' of children by subverting the hegemony of established school subjects."[44] On the secondary level, such efforts took the form of ability grouping and curriculum differentiation. Typically, educational historians have viewed such efforts to individualize educational experiences with suspicion, as part of a wider effort to fit students into the existing social order in ways that would serve capitalist interests. Efforts to select content according to the principle of "utility" appeared to be attempts to deny most pupils access to academic curricula. For some historians, a prime example of social efficiency–social control in the curriculum is found in the recommendations of the CRSE.[45] In this interpretation, subsequent to the release of the *Cardinal Principles* report, surveys became a vehicle for propagating the doctrine of social efficiency–social control.[46] Inglis served as a member of that Commission and advocated essentially identical ideas and practices in his writing. Thus, a determination of the nature and extent to which Inglis advocated ability grouping, curriculum differentiation, and utilitarian curriculum content is in order.

The brief chapter on secondary education in the Virginia survey report identified the "highly academic" character of Virginia high schools as a probable cause of low enrollments for boys and the high dropout rate.[47] The chapter called for "greater flexibility in the program of the high school" and "the introduction of more practical arts studies."[48] The proposed graduation requirements comprised "three units of English, one unit of social science, one unit of natural science, and . . . the completion of at least three units of related sequential work in some field in addition to English."[49] The Division of Tests and Measurement of the Virginia survey staff also recommended improved classification of students, use of standardized achievement and intelligence tests for the purpose of classification, differentiation of students based upon this classification, and "creation in the State Department of a bureau of educational investigation."[50] That this last set of recommendations resembles provisions that during the 1920s became hallmarks of the standardized testing movement is not surprising in light of the fact that Louis Terman and Robert Yerkes served as consultants to the Virginia survey testing program.

The purpose of the Winchester survey was to gather data to determine "the capacities, abilities, and needs of all pupils in the Winchester Schools."[51] Inglis and his colleague Walter Dearborn (a pioneer in the school survey movement) based their study on the assumption that "one of the most important reforms needed in our system of education is that of improving the present methods of class grouping and, as far as may be possible, of adapting instruction to pupils of different capacities."[52] Inglis and Dearborn administered group and individual intelligence tests and achievement tests in selected subjects to all Winchester children in grades one through eight. They also gathered information regarding teacher evaluations of tested students. Their method was essentially identical to the one employed by Terman and Yerkes in the statewide study of Virginia, although Inglis and Dearborn gave greater consideration to teacher judgments than had Terman and Yerkes.[53] Inglis and Dearborn discovered that at any grade level great disparity existed among students not only in terms of measured intelligence, but also in terms of math and language skills and most obviously in terms of chronological age. With respect to the latter, they found the range of students' chronological age at every grade level to be from six to nine years. In terms of achievement, they found, "The attempt is made to teach in the same classes advanced forms of reading to pupils whose present reading abilities range all the way from near-illiteracy to the reading abilities of the average high-school senior." They admonished, "It cannot be done."[54]

Inglis and Dearborn's recommendations were in line with contemporary notions of ability grouping.[55] They recommended classifying students into below average, average, and above average groups. At the same time, however, they called for "a more flexible system of promotion and grade classification" and advocated the promotion of "excessively over-age pupils" versus retaining them in grade as the lesser of two evils.[56] They also recommended an annual "re-classification" of all pupils in order to ensure that students were placed in groups commensurate with their development. Inglis and Dearborn hoped for "a careful adjustment of instruction to the needs and capacities [of students in] each of" the groupings. They warned that such ability groupings "will be relatively useless unless real changes are made in the instruction provided and proper adaptation is made to the needs of the different classes organized."[57]

Although subsequent research has not born out the effectiveness of ability grouping at accommodating individual needs, for the early twentieth century, Inglis and Dearborn's study of the Winchester Schools represented state-of-the-art use of standardized testing to group students by ability and aptitude for instruction.[58] The use of multiple sources of information about student learning, the provision for flexible reevaluation of groupings, and the emphasis on the imperative of tailoring instruction to individual needs were notable features of their study. Their study also reveals conditions prevalent in elementary schools at the time, which have virtually disappeared by the late twentieth century: wide disparities not only of ability, but also of age at any particular grade level. These realities may not make their faith in ability grouping any more palatable in light of subsequent research, but at least more understandable given widespread conditions they encountered.

The first major section of the survey report for Swansea presented a discussion of the purposes of public education. The report noted: "The purpose of our schools is properly considered to be the preparation of the pupils for successful participation in the life of the community of which they are most likely to become a part."[59] The report noted that although social and economic conditions recently had undergone significant change, methods of education had remained static. "Too many people have appeared to feel content in the belief that they were educating their children if they were filling their minds with an undigested mass of book knowledge with little or no regard to the application of knowledge to their work-a-day lives in the community of their actual residence."[60] The report concluded that school curricula should include "a certain amount of integrating or identical education, that is, fundamental ideas and skills that all need" complemented by content "differentiated on the basis of local needs and interests." The survey team advocated not only a curriculum more meaningful to the community, but also a system of education that would serve as a unifying force in a community susceptible, like others, to potentially divisive "sectional interests."[61]

The Swansea survey team's major findings included the fact that the proportion of students retained in grade was alarmingly high—about 40 percent. Additionally, the necessity of sending Swansea youth to the neighboring Fall River High School was found to create several problems in addition to the financial burden, namely, the inconvenience created by difficult travel discouraged students from continuing beyond grade eight, and "written entrance exams of a formal, academic type" that not only discouraged and even prevented students from continuing their education (one-fourth to one-third typically failed the exam), but also exerted undue influence on the elementary curriculum.[62] That is, under these conditions, "the content of the school curriculum in Swansea [will] be determined not by the desires of the parents, not by the needs of the children, not by the wisdom of the town's school officials, but by the subjects covered in the high school entrance examination in Fall River."[63] The new high school would offer a curriculum that devoted over 50 percent of a student's program to "common studies," with the remainder devoted to course work pertinent to his or her interests, which could include preparation for "(a) higher education in college or normal school (b) commercial and clerical occupations (c) agriculture and rural life (d) activities in the home."[64]

In Augusta, Inglis's survey staff found, among other things, that while enrollments in the elementary schools of Augusta had been stable for the previous ten years, during that same period of time enrollments at Augusta's high school had increased by over 76 percent. As he had found in Virginia, in Augusta Inglis encountered great variation of age on eleven grade levels—about one in six students under age and one in four over age. Articulation between and among elementary and secondary schools was lacking as well. Inglis's staff advocated elementary education "in which pupils are learning to control themselves and to educate themselves with the teacher as a guide and helper" instead of the traditional model "in which pupils are following the teacher, performing the tasks set by her, and learning to obey."[65] The survey staff noted progress in Augusta's elementary schools toward this preferred form, and called for perseverance in continuing such efforts. In order to continue such efforts, the staff recommended "intelligent use of what is called the 'socialized' type of school activity, and . . . the 'problem' method of instruction."[66] The staff found that while most pupils remained in school until fifteen years of age, by age sixteen more than half left school. Inglis surmised that this exodus was due to the fact that "curricula have not yet been properly adjusted to their [students'] needs."[67] Inglis reported that the emphasis in high school was squarely on college preparation, although no more that 3.5 percent of students continued on to college.

The survey staff recommended that the Augusta schools adopt the "Six-Three-Three Plan" of grade level organization. Recognizing that such reorganization could expediently be limited to "building and grade adjustments," the staff emphasized that the "real reorganization" involved "educational materials and methods." Genuine reorganization would include the implementation of "a more gradual transition from practices which are characteristic of elementary education to those which are characteristic of secondary education." These practices included "gradual changes in subject matter, methods, discipline, and internal administration." The staff also called for a "reduction of review work," "the elimination of relatively less useful materials for those of greater worth," "the abolition of formalism," "earlier and better provision for individual differences" (through diagnostic testing), "subordination of deferred values" to interests of immediate relevance to school work, and accommodation of the reality that "many pupils will not be able to continue their education through the full secondary-school course."[68] The staff cautioned against the tendency to organize the junior high school into "definitely separated curricula" such as academic, commercial, and industrial courses. The staff warned that such an approach could lead "to a very undesirable practice of premature fixation of vocational interests." The staff concluded, "[t]he junior high school is distinctly an institution characterized by opportunity for educational and vocational diagnosis and guidance—not for vocational training."[69] The staff indicated that these recommendations were consistent with the recommendations of the CRSE. These recommendations were also consistent with Inglis's earlier recommendations for the junior high school and the senior high school.[70]

Inglis investigated instruction in Indiana high schools by administering standardized tests in reading and algebra and by visiting classrooms. He concluded that "observation and tests concur in showing that the larger high schools of the state are doing more satisfactory work, but that the work of the smaller high schools is very unsatisfactory."[71] Inglis observed that small high schools typically staffed less experienced and poorly prepared teachers. He reported:

> The inevitable result is a mechanical type of instruction, which emphasizes the absorption of information by the pupil, and the repetition in class of "what the textbook says" in response to questions which call for the words of the book instead of an understanding of the fact, principle, or law involved. The importance of facts is not

> to be denied, but the learning of facts and the acquisition of information are relatively ineffective unless relationships are understood and unless the pupil works the material learned into his own system of thinking. The high school should aim to develop ability to use facts and principles, not merely to reproduce words.[72]

Inglis identified the function of the standardized tests as "to determine the efficiency of instruction" in algebra and reading.[73] Significantly, instruction that focused on sheer recall of facts, or verbalism, at the expense of developing the ability to apply them, Inglis considered inefficient. Thus, the term *efficient* in this sense connotes not economy so much as effectiveness or competence, and avoids the miseducative effects of the "cult of efficiency" that Callahan detested.

Inglis found Indiana high school requirements "too academic." At first glance this finding seems to support allegations advanced recently by scholars that progressive educators believed that many, if not most, students were incapable of rigorous academic work, which led in turn to a dilution of the secondary curriculum.[74] The emphasis in these passages is not upon student ability or any lack thereof, but upon the ways in which "subjects as ordinarily organized and taught" were or were not accessible to nonacademically oriented students. Formalistic, academic treatment of knowledge characteristic of the verbalism that Inglis condemned, and which apparently dominated schooling at that time (and to a great extent still does), presented students with more of an endurance test than with opportunities for genuine learning. Curriculum and instruction that was "too academic" or that was "formal" was not accessible to all youth. Inglis had first-hand observations of classroom instruction and test scores to verify these claims.

In his survey of vocational education in Indiana, Inglis found that regulations required that students could enroll in vocational courses only if at least half of their program was devoted to vocational offerings. Such a regulation, in an attempt to meet federal funding stipulations, clearly differentiated curriculum for vocational students and, considering the separation of vocational and academic curriculum in Indiana at the time, would constitute a rigid form of tracking—indeed almost a dual system. Thus Inglis implored:

> All girls should have at least the opportunity for some contact with home economics, but not all girls should be expected to devote one-half of their time to its intensive study.... This is wrong. There is no sound educational reason why a girl should not take some single course in cooking, sewing, or other home economics course for which she is fitted, without being obliged to devote one half of her study to intensive work in vocational and related subject in this field.[75]

Similarly,

> Every country boy or girl should have the opportunity to take some work in agriculture without necessarily devoting one half of his time to its intensive study.[76]

Inglis therefore recommended

> the abandonment in small high schools of the half-day or none policy, and the organization of vocational work on the class-unit basis rather than on the full departmental basis . . . It means only a different administrative organization which would permit a wider sphere of influence for vocational education and broader opportunities for pupils in the small high school.[77]

As had other surveys in which Inglis participated, the Indiana survey called for institution of the 6–3–3 plan and included as models for the state to consider several suggested consolidation and reorganization plans.

Finally, the treatment of matters of race in the Virginia survey warrants attention. Although the report dedicated a separate chapter to "Negro Education in Virginia," throughout the report the survey staff described and discussed the education of white and African American children together. The survey staff's recognition in passing that "separate schools must be maintained for white and colored children" no doubt referred to de jure segregation at the time prevalent in the American South.[78] Similarly, the survey staff's observation that "the principle of racial integrity is fundamental in the minds of both races," reflects euphemistically the widespread pre–*Brown v. Board* notion of coexisting, "separate but equal" facilities for blacks and whites.[79] In contrast to the emphasis on social "intermingling" and "unification" advocated by the CRSE and by Inglis in *Principles*, the recommendations of the Virginia survey stopped well short of extending this kind of association to African Americans, at least in that southern state, a contradiction widespread among progressive reformers.[80] To be sure, the survey staff did not explicitly challenge these entrenched cultural mores of Virginia in 1919.

Yet the report contains observations and statements that likely provoked some discomfort for white and perhaps even African American leaders in the state. The survey staff, for example, reported the following:

> In 1916, according to the figures of the Federal Bureau of Education, Virginia stood thirty-second among the States of the Union with respect to the proportion of the total population attending high school and thirty-fourth with respect to the proportion of pupils enrolled attending high school. It must be remembered, however, that the large negro population in Virginia renders any such comparison misleading, since the

> economic and social status of the negroes precludes any very large negro enrollment in the high school even if ample facilities were provided. Among the Southern States Virginia easily stands in the first place with respect to the proportions of the total populations of the school enrollment attending the high school.[81]

This statement at once highlighted low national ranking for the state (something that would likely embarrass state leaders), attributed Virginia's low national standing to African Americans (something with which white leaders would likely agree), and exposed the low socioeconomic standing to which African Americans were kept (something that white leaders could not deny, but in this context served as the cause of the low state ranking) as it ranked Virginia as a leader among states in the South. Without making too much of the passage, it does embed a recognition of inequality in the context of an appeal to regional identity and even pride. In a discussion of the results of assessments administered as part of the survey, the survey staff presented statistics that suggested that "the apparent differences are not very great between the achievements of colored children and those of white children."[82] The qualification, "[i]t must be remembered, however, that in almost every grade considered colored pupils are on the average a year or more older and have attended school on the average of a year longer than the white pupils," may well have been included as much in the interest of discretion as of description.[83] Looking back from the early twentieth-first century, it is well to recall that these statements were made at a time when not even scholarly opinion, never mind popular opinion, had yet significantly separated race and intelligence as causal factors, though Inglis had already reached this conclusion.

Again, evidence of the disparity between educational conditions for blacks and whites pervades the Virginia survey report, not only as represented in statistical data, but also as documented in photographs that appeared throughout.[84] The commission noted, "While the improvement in recent years has been noticeable and in a few features rather remarkable, yet on the whole, the situation of the Negro schools is far from satisfactory. They suffer from the same defects as noted in the case of the schools for white children, but to a more serious degree."[85] The survey staff recommended improvements to the education of African Americans which, while retaining mandatory "racial integrity," if implemented would effectively place the schooling of African Americans on a par with the schooling of whites in Virginia. The survey staff recommended enhancements to virtually every aspect of African American education, from the training and compensation of African American teachers, to the conditions and equipment of schools, to courses of study, to the improvement of roads so that African American children could get to school. They recommended more "colored supervisors" to assist African American teachers than white supervisors to assist white teachers. They recommended that funding of African American schools increase as needed to implement such improvements. The survey staff portrayed the effective separate coexistence of the races as inherently dependent upon the well-being of each. The staff claimed, for example,

> The prosperity of the colored farmers means the prosperity of the white farmers as well, the prosperity of merchants and manufacturers, bankers and business men of the entire state. It means increasing the taxable wealth and building up the very foundation for good schools, good roads, churches, and all community undertakings for the general welfare of the people.[86]

The following statement is representative of the survey staff's position on the education of African Americans in Virginia in 1919:

> It is not to be expected that at present the ratio of pupils in high school grades should be the same for the white and colored population, for the time a pupil can spend in school depends on the economic and social conditions of the home from which he comes, as well as upon the general desire for knowledge on the part of the students, and colored people are not as favorably situated as white people in this respect. Most of the rural high schools for white children have been established within the last fifteen years, and the time is now ripe to do more for the high school training of colored children.[87]

Echoing the survey staff's recommendations, the Virginia Education Commission also depicted the improvement of education and of other conditions for African Americans as in the interests of whites. In what could have been taken as alarmist language, the commission warned, "To entrust these [African American] children to slip-shod and haphazard instruction is dangerous."[88] The Virginia surveyors exploited contemporary fears of racial conflict in order to argue for increasingly equitable, albeit still separate, educational facilities for African American students.

As director of the Virginia survey Inglis had a large hand in shaping the final report. Most significant, however, is the resemblance of the recommendations for improving the education of African Americans in Virginia and the position on the influence of race on intelligence and personal potential that Inglis had stated in *Principles*. The recommendations contained in the survey report clearly echo Inglis's previous position on these issues. Consistent with progressives at large, the authors of the Virginia survey accepted de facto and de jure segregation of African Americans and whites. The Virginia survey authors, however, did not accept the educational inequalities that resulted from segregation. Contrary to contemporary trends in the South "to send an unmistakable message of racial inequality that would intimidate blacks and reassure whites" and "to deprive blacks of so much economic and political opportunity that they could never threaten white power," Inglis's survey of public education in Virginia recommended that the improvement of African American schools toward racial equality in education represented a positive step toward preventing racial and social conflict.[89] Inglis and his survey team recommended vast improvements to the education of African Americans in Virginia at a time when the policy of southern white leadership and northern philanthropists toward the education of African Americans had yet to begin a shift from neglect to support.[90]

In summary then, with respect to the educational dimensions of his survey work, Inglis found that academic formalism, by demanding from students work that was largely remote from and therefore meaningless both to their present circumstances and to their future aspirations, effectively undermined educational quality and opportunity. To improve educational quality and opportunity, Inglis recommended (1) organization of curriculum and methods of the junior high school so that institution would serve as a transition between elementary and secondary school that would mitigate against "elimination" of students; (2) devotion of about half of the high school curriculum to common (academic) requirements and half to electives that served student interests, aptitudes, and aspirations; (3) ability grouping designed to accommodate individual differences that was sufficiently flexible and included periodic "re-classification" of students' placements; and (4) alternative methods of instruction that would make subject matter accessible to all students. Additionally, Inglis warned against the tendency for differentiated curricula to isolate students from one another and emphasized the unifying function of public education. All of these reforms were among the recommendations of the CRSE, of which Inglis, again, was a member.[91] In short, although Inglis's recommendations resembled the kinds of reforms that late twentieth-century historians associated with social efficiency–social control ideology in name, they did not precisely conform to that depiction and, in fact, in substance they departed from it in significant ways.

Understanding the Inglis Surveys

An examination of Inglis's survey work reveals not only both consistencies and inconsistencies between his survey work and historians' characterizations of the survey movement, but also that the inconsistencies are not minor. Inglis tailored the recommendations that emerged from his survey work to unique local circumstances and needs; put another way, his analyses and recommendations were always situational. Although the Inglis surveys manifest concern for economy and cost effectiveness, this concern came not at the expense of but, rather, in the interest of increasing educational quality and opportunity. Although Inglis took the existing bureaucratic organization for granted, he considered it a vehicle for improving educational programs that was responsive to local needs and interests. In addition, although the Inglis surveys represent an effort to disseminate the kinds of principles and practices advocated by the CRSE, Inglis's recommendations reveal something other than a narrow conception of social efficiency and social control. Thus, Inglis's work is inconsistent with important aspects of the economic, organizational, and educational dimensions of the social efficiency interpretation of the survey movement to the extent that it often contradicts that thesis. Prevailing interpretations of the survey movement, then, seem to offer inadequate explanations of Inglis's survey work.

Inglis's survey work is consistent with three aspects of existing historical interpretations of the survey movement. One is Callahan's observation that "the outlooks and competence of the surveyors influenced the nature of the survey," which leaves room for the existence of significant nuances in the survey movement, nuances—even anomalies—that appear, for example, in Inglis's survey work. Another is the clear consistency of Inglis's survey work with Lagemann's identification of surveys with efforts to create a "science" of education based upon an expanding base of "school facts." Indeed, Inglis's survey work manifests the increasing respect for evidence-based decision making in education that historians writing before 1960 emphasized. A third is the similarity between many of the recommendations in Inglis's survey work and Tyack's profile of "pedagogical progressives," a group usually overshadowed by attention to the "administrative progressives."[92] Despite these similarities, however, the discrepancies between the Inglis surveys and the prevailing social efficiency–social control interpretation are nevertheless remarkable.

As noted, historians portray school surveys as vehicles for advocating proposals in the *Cardinal Principles* report. Yet although most historical interpretations depict the proposals outlined in the *Cardinal Principles* report as antisubject matter, for Inglis the intent of those proposals was to mitigate the miseducative effects of academic formalism by encouraging not the abandonment of but the application of subject matter. Virtually obscured in late twentieth-century historical scholarship is the early twentieth-century conception of the junior high school as a transition between elementary and secondary education such as Inglis promoted. If these kinds of recommendations appear with sufficient frequency in other surveys and generally in the work of Inglis's contemporaries, then it could be that the work of pedagogical progressives like Inglis has been underrepresented. At the very least, surveys remain a largely untapped source of data about early twentieth-century education in the United States. In any event, the principles of secondary education that Inglis advocated in his 1918 book, in journal articles, and on the CRSE, appear in sharper relief in his school survey work. Inglis's commitment to some educational practices associated with "pedagogical progressives" is manifest in his survey work, and would become increasingly apparent in his work during the early 1920s.

CHAPTER SIX

Full Progressive

During the early 1920s, Alexander Inglis attained the full measure of his professional capacity and influence, in terms both of his professional rank and status and of his engagement with progressive education initiatives. His commitment to progressive principles remained strong while his professional interests, which he approached as opportunities to apply and advocate those principles, continued to expand. As an outgrowth of his school surveying, Inglis began to develop intelligence quotient scales and achievement tests for English vocabulary and for Latin. He weighed in on a popular proposal to expand the role of the federal Bureau of Education and continued to write about the reform of secondary education. He revisited classical pedagogy to argue for the application of progressive principles of teaching and learning to Latin instruction. He summarized the last quarter century of developments in secondary education in the United States and identified challenges for achieving fully the new functions of the high school. Inglis remained active both in his responsibilities to building the program in secondary education at the Harvard Graduate School of Education and in professional service. In short, during the early 1920s, Inglis hit his full stride, so to speak, as a progressive educator.

Campus Duties and Professional Responsibilities

By 1920, Inglis's teaching assignment at Harvard had expanded along with the program in secondary education; from 1920 to 1923 he taught the following graduate courses: during the fall semester, Principles of Secondary Education and Historical and Comparative Study of Secondary Education; during the spring semester, Principles of Teaching in the Secondary School and the Junior High School and Plans for the Reorganization of Secondary Education; and during both fall and spring semesters, Problems of Secondary Education and Tests and Scales for the Secondary School, as well as Supervision of Independent Research. By 1920, Bancroft Beatley, Inglis's doctoral student, had assumed responsibility for Apprentice Teaching in the Secondary School and for two undergraduate courses for prospective teachers. During the 1923–4 academic year, Inglis added to his schedule a new course about Secondary-School Administration and cotaught Problems of Secondary Education and Tests and Scales for the Secondary School with Beatley. Then an assistant professor in the Harvard Graduate School of Education, Beatley assumed more of Inglis's teaching load, including the fall section of Principles of Secondary Education and Principles of Teaching in the Secondary School. Harvard's program in secondary education had expanded not only with the addition of Inglis's new course, but also with a new course on the Organization and Administration of Extracurricular Activities in Secondary Schools and with the appointment of two new faculty, George Ellsworth Johnson and William M. Proctor, the latter visiting from Stanford University.[1]

Course descriptions from the catalog of the Graduate School of Education indicate that the topics Inglis covered in his classes paralleled the content of *Principles of Secondary Education* and involved examination and critique of contemporary practices and trends in and proposals for secondary education. Principles of Secondary Education, the prerequisite for all courses in the secondary education program, was "designed to introduce the student into the scientific study of secondary education." This course included a field component that would, through "[v]isits to comprehensive high schools of different sizes and types, technical schools, vocational schools for girls, vocational schools for boys, commercial high schools, trade schools, continuation schools, part-time cooperative schools, schools for retail selling an store service, college preparatory schools, junior and senior high schools, enable the student to acquaint himself with all forms of secondary education by direct and personal contact."[2] Problems of Secondary Education began with "a general resume of the more important problems affecting secondary education at the present day with particular reference to plans for the reorganization of secondary education as outlined by the National Commission on the Reorganization of Secondary Education," and proceeded with student research into selected problems. Tests and Scales for the Secondary School was "designed as a laboratory course for the development of standard tests and scales for the measurement of instruction in junior and senior high schools," and involved students in "the application of existing tests and the development of new tests and scales."[3] Course descriptions indicate that Inglis's teaching and research each informed the other.

Just two sources suggest Inglis's qualities as a teacher. In a brief address at the memorial meeting held by the Harvard Graduate School of Education, his student Frank Lee Wright, characterized Inglis's classroom as infused with a "sense of humor and eager enthusiasm." Wright claimed that Inglis "was most effective in stimulating thought," emphasizing that Inglis "never demanded agreement with his ideas, but he did demand that we be able to defend our own ideas." Inglis expected persistence from his students and was exceptional at pushing students to their "best efforts." At the same time, Inglis was known by students as a sympathetic friend: "Many a student will remember the delightful, stimulating, friendly chats on the stairways in old Lawrence Hall," Wright concluded.[4] In an unpublished memoir, L. Thomas Hopkins recalled that Inglis began his seminar by assuring students that "this was not a lecture but a discussion course, that everyone was free to participate as he wished, and that there would be no answers imposed by the professor."[5] Hopkins continued, "My opportunities to chat with him informally came at the education library after ten o'clock at night when it had closed for the day. He came in to study and think during the quiet hours." On these occasions, Hopkins and Inglis would often "go out for a midnight walk and [not] return to work until two in the morning." Hopkins described Inglis as a "tall, thin man with a heavy chest voice and a slow manner of speaking, [who] conveyed the appearance of giving deep thought to each of his communications."[6]

When surveying commitments drew Inglis off campus for extended periods of time, he remained in regular contact with his dean and good friend Harry Holmes, who often covered Inglis's teaching assignments. For example, throughout his stint surveying the Virginia system of education, Inglis corresponded with Holmes about matters pertaining to Harvard's Division of Education, as well as to personal concerns. During the spring 1919 semester, Holmes taught Inglis's courses. Holmes offered, "I am having great fun with your courses . . . and shall really hate to give Education 9 back to you." He continued, "I find teaching from your book extremely satisfactory, perhaps largely because you give such a splendid basis of facts, so that I can soar of into interpretations at will. Mostly," Holmes concluded, "I agree with you, but sometimes not."[7] Inglis promptly and characteristically replied to Holmes, "Glad you are enjoying the courses. It shocks me to learn that you do not agree with me on every point in the tome."[8]

Plans for the reorganization of the Division of Education into the Graduate School of Education and the prospect of Inglis's promotion to full professor, however, characterized the bulk of the correspondence between the two men. In fact, these matters were inextricably interrelated. Despite Holmes's extremely favorable recommendation for Inglis's advancement, coupled with what appears to have been a plea that persisted nearly to the point of forwardness, President Lowell decided to delay Inglis's promotion until approval by the Harvard Corporation of the plan for the new graduate school. This approval hinged upon a grant from the General Education Board, which, after considerable maneuvering on the part of Holmes and Hanus, was awarded in 1919.[9]

In his letter to Lowell arguing Inglis's case for promotion to the rank of professor, Holmes characterized Inglis as "one of the most helpful, constructive, and reliable participators in all our Division activities." Holmes claimed that Inglis's "reputation in his field has advanced steadily, so that it is now fair to say that he is the leading authority in this country on Secondary Education." Holmes reported on a survey in the Monograph of the Society of College Teachers of Education that found that *Principles* "is used in University courses on Secondary Education more often than any two out of a list of twenty-seven" other books. After recognizing the "large part" Inglis had "in formulating [the] highly important report" of the Commission on the Reorganization of Secondary Education and Inglis's participation in school surveys, Holmes reported that "during his service with us he has twice refused to be considered for higher posts in other universities, in one case for the directorship of the School of Education at the University of Illinois."[10]

Writing to Inglis in Virginia, Holmes reported, "I argued as long and hard as I could, but the President was firm in his stand that we ought to wait until we got the school." Holmes added assuredly, "He had nothing whatever to say on the merits of the case and agreed entirely as to the increase in salary, although he would not discuss the precise amount."[11] Inglis replied with characteristic grace, "I can easily understand the position which President Lowell assumed. I know that you personally and the Division did everything within your power and I appreciate it sincerely."[12] A few weeks later, Holmes was able to report to Inglis "positively that if the Graduate plans go through, and when they go through, the professorship will be offered to you."[13] A year later, Holmes telegrammed Inglis, who was vacationing at Camp Grant in Rockford, Illinois, with the news, "Corporation appointed you full professor. Overseers must confirm. Hallelujah!"[14]

During the years after his promotion to the rank of professor, Inglis's governance responsibilities at the Harvard Graduate School of Education included service as chair of the Standing Committee on Publications, as member of the Standing Committee on Appointments, and in 1923–4 as member of the Standing Committee on Admissions. Over his ten years in Cambridge, Inglis taught his courses for both Harvard's Division and, after 1920, Graduate School of Education, and also at Radcliffe College, as noted earlier. Inglis also contributed to the opening of the Graduate School of Education to women upon its founding in 1920.[15]

At the top of his career, Inglis faced no shortage of opportunities for professional service. In 1921, for example, he served as a headhunter for an unnamed high school searching for a new principal, and in the process solicited recommendations from the likes of Jesse Newlon, Charles Judd, and Ellwood Cubberley. Inglis declined an invitation to teach during the 1923 summer session at the University of California at Berkeley, but accepted such an invitation for the summer of 1926. He declined an invitation to conduct a survey of the Valparaiso schools in March 1924, and in early April 1924 offered suggestions to a presidential search at Wesleyan University.[16]

Figure 6.1. The faculty of the Harvard Graduate School of Education, 1921. *Standing*: George E. Johnson, Bancroft Beatley, Alexander J. Inglis, John M. Brewer, Edward A. Lincoln, L. O. Cummings. *Seated*: Edwin A. Shaw, Walter F. Dearborn, Paul H. Hanus, Henry W. Holmes, Lewis A. Maverick. Courtesy of Special Collections, Monroe C. Gutman Library, Harvard University Graduate School of Education.

During this time, Inglis became increasingly active in professional associations and learned societies. He had become a member of the American Association for the Advancement of Science in 1911 and had been elected a fellow by the association's council in 1913. He also maintained membership with the NEA, National Society for the Study of Education, New England Association of Colleges and Secondary Schools, and the National Association of Directors of Educational Research. His social memberships included the Harvard, Boston City, and University Clubs.[17] His most active professional memberships appear to have been with the Cleveland Conference and the Society of College Teachers of Education.

The National Society of College Teachers of Education (NSCTE) emerged in 1902 from a meeting of the NEA's Department of Superintendence "to give consideration to problems of organization and methods of instruction in collegiate and university departments of education."[18] Early chairmen (a role later designated president) included Charles DeGarmo, John Dewey, and James

E. Russell, president of Teachers College, Columbia University. Presidents who preceded Inglis included Paul Hanus, Charles Judd, W. W. Charters, and William Bagley. By 1919 the NSCTE included 243 members. In 1911, the NSCTE began publishing an annual yearbook, which contained conference papers and discussions. Inglis served as president of NSCTE in 1922.[19]

Inglis also enjoyed membership in the Cleveland Conference, one of the "networks" that Tyack and Hansot have characterized as something of a backroom "old-boy" club that served more to enhance the power and status of its members than to contribute to the improvement of schooling.[20] Initially formed as a study group in 1915 from a meeting held by Leonard Ayers following his completion of a survey of the Cleveland schools, the Cleveland Conference held its first regular meeting in 1916; attendees included Leonard Ayers, Ellwood P. Cubberley, Paul Hanus, Charles Judd, and Paul Monroe. Meetings were devoted to discussion of a wide range of educational problems of the day, which literally numbered in the dozens and included nearly every imaginable major and minor contemporary issue, defying easy characterization. Members recommended individuals for invitation to membership; absenteeism from meetings resulted in removal from membership. During the early 1920s, meetings typically occurred in February and December of each year and were held in Cleveland or Chicago. The Cleveland Conference invited Inglis to membership in 1918. Due to wartime exigencies, no meeting occurred in 1919, and records indicate that Inglis was absent from the 1920 and 1921 meetings, but that he attended the December 1922 meeting in Chicago. Inglis's name, however, did not appear on the 1923 membership list.[21]

In short, by the early 1920s, Inglis was fully engaged with the expanding work of the Harvard Graduate School of Education, particularly with the program in secondary education, continually enjoyed opportunities for profession service, and was ensconced in influential professional networks of progressive educators. Inglis was by no means, however, in complete accord with every educational trend of his day.

The Federal Role in Education

Among the major contemporary issues that the Cleveland Conference discussed during the years of Inglis's membership was a proposal to enhance the status of the federal Bureau of Education. The Cleveland Conference maintained no records of actual discussions other than topics considered; Inglis, however, weighed in on this issue outside of the conference. The NEA had long lobbied for increased federal aid to education, but largely in the form of research and information dissemination. Around 1920, however, the NEA launched a campaign to elevate the federal

Bureau of Education to cabinet status. Between 1919 and 1925 a series of bills proposed to Congress sought not only increased appropriations, but also cabinet status for the bureau. Although support of such a reorganization of federal agencies was not unanimous, even within the NEA, it was widespread among educators.[22] Inglis, however, opposed it vigorously.

Inglis addressed one iteration of the proposal, the Smith-Towner Bill.[23] Inglis objected to the bill on the grounds that it represented unsound government policy, that it was dangerous for public education, that it was bad economic policy, and that it was simply unfair. Federal subsidy for education was "bad governmental policy" because federal money would be followed by federal control of its use. Inglis characterized federal interference with state and local policies as "intolerable." In his survey work, particularly in Indiana, Inglis had discerned such effects from the Smith-Hughes Act. He summarized, "Let us not be deceived. All acts providing for federal subsidies in aid of education carry with them the dynamite of federal participation in the control of education and the determination of educational policies."[24] Federal subsidy to education "interferes with the proper development of education itself" because the "paternalism" that it engenders has "an inevitable tendency to result ultimately in a lowering of the educational morale of the local public through the lessening of local initiative, interest, and responsibility."[25]

For Inglis, federal subsidy of education represented "bad economic policy" because "wastefulness in the expenditure of public funds is in direct proportion to the remoteness of the appropriating agency from the source of supply."[26] Finally, federal subsidies for education "are essentially unfair . . . not because they operate to equalize the burdens of educational support but because they fail utterly to accomplish that end or even to attempt it." This was largely because monies are typically distributed on the "basis of population distribution" rather than "with reference to demonstrated [educational] needs."[27] Inglis recognized that severe educational problems awaited resolution—as he had documented in his survey work—but insisted that resolution would result from state and local resolve, rather than from federal meddling.

For Inglis, reorganization of federal agencies was important only so far as it enabled their proper functioning; their proper functions were not political, as he feared cabinet status for a federal education agency would make them, but professional, that is, scientific and technical. In short, without evoking a constitutional argument, Inglis asserted that the cabinet status of an education department proposed in the Towner-Sterling Bill would threaten state and local control of public education. Inglis was not alone in his criticisms, but among educators he voiced a minority opinion. In the short run, at least, Inglis's view prevailed, though not for the reasons he advocated. Although the NEA would continue to express support for such a measure until the creation of the Department of Health, Education, and Welfare in 1953, by 1930, as support from constituents outside NEA dwindled, any chances for immediate success had passed.

Testing

During the early 1920s, Inglis began work on various aspects of intelligence and achievement testing. During World War I, psychologists developed "group testing" methods in order to identify more efficiently aptitudes of recruits and better place them in roles in which they could make the greatest contribution to the war effort.[28] Inglis was probably aware of such efforts from his wartime temporary assignment with the War Department's Committee on Education and Special Training, which, as noted, placed military personnel in training programs conducted by civilian institutions. And as director of the survey of the educational system of the state of Virginia after the war, Inglis had associated with Robert Yerkes and Louis Terman, two psychologists who subsequently campaigned vigorously to introduce group or standardized testing to the public schools. Inglis generated his *Intelligence Quotient Values* in 1921 and *English Vocabulary Tests* in 1923.[29] Inglis also contributed to what was apparently a university-wide project to develop a bank of tests for numerous subjects, called The Harvard Tests, by constructing instruments to assess achievement in Latin morphology, Latin syntax, and Latin vocabulary.[30] Apparently, students in Inglis's Tests and Scales for the Secondary School course collaborated in the development of these tests.[31]

In an article published in *The English Leaflet*, Inglis described how he had developed the high school English vocabulary test.[32] Using the vocabulary frequency study of Godfrey Dewey, Inglis classified English vocabulary into three categories: commonly used vocabulary, specialized vocabulary, and vocabulary of "the intelligent general reader." He reported that most persons used very little vocabulary beyond the common and specialized categories. Because the role of the school was to prepare students to become "intelligent general readers," Inglis constructed a test of vocabulary from this third category "to determine the *reading* vocabulary of the student."[33] The article described the construction of the tests, several forms and scoring procedures, and suggested possible uses for educators. For Inglis such tests were tools that could aid educators in arriving at "a definite knowledge of the existing status of the educand."[34] The results could be used for diagnostics, placement, accommodating individual differences, grading, and following individual improvement. Inglis's test work manifests many of the features of the testing movement of his day, including its optimism. In the context of Inglis's recognition of the limitations of such data, however, his approach may have avoided some of the wider movement's excesses.

Although Inglis developed intelligence quotient scales and Latin achievement tests and recommended their use to school systems, as well as deployed standardized tests in school surveys, he did not publish the kind of systematic analysis of the theory and research on testing that he previously had applied, for example, to secondary education and to the role of federal education agencies, and subsequently to Latin pedagogy. Thus, Inglis left no comprehensive theory of testing of his own. The little he wrote about the uses of a test he developed—about three paragraphs—was mostly a summary of recognized contemporary uses.[35] Although in this summary he identified classification, grading, and even employment selection among the possible uses of his vocabulary test, he emphasized its diagnostic power for improving the teaching and learning of individual students. His recommendations for using tests in his surveys also focused on accommodating individual differences, emphasized flexible classification arrangements, and were premised on the position that grouping students by ability "will be relatively useless unless real changes are made in the instruction provided." This emphasis was consistent with his interest in the importance of accommodating individual differences and the inadvisability of rigid curriculum differentiation.[36]

For Inglis, then, tests served primarily as instructional tools that would enable the adjustment of instruction to individual needs. He was interested in classification of students only to the extent that it led to improvements in instruction and in learning. Put another way, Inglis was less committed to the administrative than to the pedagogical use of tests. Although the use of tests to classify students can be associated with administrative progressives' commitment to efficient differentiation of pupils, pedagogical progressives embraced the instructional potential of testing. Indeed, even John Dewey, who unlike Inglis sharply criticized the use of tests for classification of pupils, nevertheless recognized the potential pedagogical value of standardized testing.[37]

Progressive Classicism

On 1 June 1922, in a note to Andrew West, dean of Graduate Studies at Princeton University and a powerful leader in the classicist community, Inglis wrote about *Principles of Secondary Education*, a copy of which he had sent to West, "Try not to believe it all inasmuch as the wisdom of a few years has made me doubt myself much of what I have committed myself to in black and white."[38] Recall that in both his doctoral dissertation and in *Principles of Secondary Education*, Inglis had effectively repudiated his initial professional commitment to the classics. Based upon the utility criterion, Inglis saw a severely curtailed place for the classics in the modern high school curriculum.[39] West, for whom virtually every political, social, and economic development signaled the continuing value of the classics to modern life, likely would have recoiled at such a suggestion.[40] On Saturday, 16 September 1922, Inglis and West met in Manhattan to discuss The Classical Investigation, a national study of classical pedagogy in American high schools conducted by the American Classical League with support from the General Education Board. Ultimately, Inglis would not participate in the Classical Investigation, although the final report would draw from his work.[41] But Inglis's note to West perhaps suggests that Inglis may have entertained second thoughts about his critique of conventional classical pedagogy and its place in the high school curriculum.

Recall also that the early twentieth century was an exasperating time for classicists. Not only was the value of the classics in the school curriculum and to contemporary life constantly under siege, but also enrollments seemed simultaneously to wax and wane. Contemporary educational theory, such as that advanced by Inglis and by Abraham Flexner accorded the classics little relevance for modern life and prescribed for them an increasingly diminished role in the curriculum. Although from 1890 to 1920 the percentage of 14–17-year-olds enrolled in public high schools increased nearly six-fold, from 5.6 percent to 31.2 percent, the proportion of the total enrollments in Latin by 1922 (27.52 percent) was below 1890 levels (34.69 percent)—and still falling (by 1934 to 16.04 percent). At the same time, due to the increase in the proportion of adolescents enrolled in school, though the proportion of enrollments in Latin declined, the real number of students in Latin classes increased dramatically, nearly doubling between 1910 and 1934, from 362,548 to 721,320. Classicists faced the unnerving paradox of concurrent decline and expansion of enrollments in their discipline.[42]

In an article originally read in 1922 at the Third Annual Meeting of the American Classical League, Inglis argued that the expansion of secondary school enrollments and an accompanying democratization of the high school, along with a shift in "our philosophy of secondary education" from "a theory of selection for leadership to a theory which postulates that educational opportunities should be provided for each citizen according to his capacities and needs," held profound implications for all subjects, including the classics.[43] He observed that traditional approaches to classical pedagogy were appropriate for the "relatively homogeneous group" of "relatively [academically] superior pupils" who "looked forward to higher education or desired the sort of an education which was represented by preparation for college."[44] Inglis suggested that while traditional pedagogy appeared to work for traditional students, the expansion and diversification of the pupil population necessitated a wider range of approaches to curriculum and instruction. The danger for classical pedagogy was "that it tends to resist modification and to retain a rigidly organized methodology not well suited to conditions different from those which it was originally developed to meet."[45] Inglis maintained, therefore, that classical pedagogy must change to accommodate the new educational circumstances wrought largely by demographic changes in school enrollments.

Inglis contended that, in order to reach all students successfully, classical instruction must meet three conditions. The first condition was "that instruction be adapted to the capacities and needs of the pupils concerned in any case." Inglis maintained that "methods of classical instruction as at present commonly organized practically exclude a very large proportion of secondary school pupils from successful study of the Classics."[46] Inglis reasoned that, because no evidence was available to indicate that Latin and Greek were mastered only by academically elite Romans and Greeks, "it is perfectly possible for any pupil in the secondary school" during the early twentieth century to learn these languages.[47] Inglis criticized classics teachers of his day for failing to modify their methods of instruction in order to reach more students. "The supremacy of the subject must give way to the supremacy of the pupil, if instruction is to be successful," he exhorted.[48] In practice, this meant studying "the capacities, interests, and needs of each class and, as far as possible, of each pupil in each class" as a prerequisite to developing "new methods of classical instruction" that "must vary somewhat according to the character of the pupils concerned."[49]

The conformity of classical pedagogy to the "laws of learning" was the second condition Inglis set. He noted that the recent "practical recognition of the fact that successful learning is determined primarily by the psychology of the learner rather than by the logical relations of subject matter as viewed by the expert acquainted with the subject in its complete form" was veritably ignored in classical pedagogy.[50] Laws of learning that recognized the importance of developing "motivational interests," of building upon previous learning, and of retention were ignored, at best, and "violated constantly," at worst, in contemporary classical instruction.[51] As examples, Inglis noted that the remoteness of classical study from students' immediate experience (save those intent on meeting college entrance requirements) manifested a failure of classical pedagogy to attend to "motivating interests." Inglis suggested that the tendency to lump "such formal elements as morphology, syntax, and vocabulary in the first year of instruction" with opportunities for application in reading and writing contexts postponed, violated the principle that mastery results from use.[52]

The third condition Inglis set for the success of classical pedagogy was that it "be so organized as to make its maximum contribution to the attainment of those aims and values for which the classical languages and literatures are studied."[53] At this point, for Inglis the question of the appropriate place of Latin in the school curriculum was overshadowed by the fact that an increasing number and proportion of adolescents were enrolled in classics courses. In addition to "habits of mental work, ideals of thoroughness, ideals of accuracy and precision of thought, and attitudes toward study and intellectual achievement" (all of which he conceded could be cultivated in any subject), Inglis identified "the development of general linguistic ability" and "the development of social-cultural understanding and interest" as values of study of the classics that should be expressly pursued, rather than merely assumed, in classical curriculum and instruction.[54] This meant elimination of "a deadening formalism of instruction" and of mere "linguistic gymnastics, empty of content and devoid of interest" that classics instructors often mistook for academic rigor.[55]

In his summary, Inglis asserted that the three conditions that classical instruction must meet for success applied equally to any and all subjects. Avoiding the dualistic extremism of opponents who advocated the omission and proponents who championed the omniscience of Latin as a school subject, Inglis in effect extended his earlier discussion of the place of Latin in the curriculum by calling for the application of progressive principles of teaching to Latin pedagogy. Although Inglis did not see the classics occupying a large place in the curriculum, he recognized that as larger numbers of students enrolled in the subject, new methods would be required to reach these diverse students. Inglis would have the classics taught in such a fashion that made the experience educative, rather than merely a formality, for a wider range of students. Rather than significantly changing his position on the classics, as his note to Andrew West may have implied he had done, Inglis instead advocated applying the principles of learning he previously had advocated for other subjects to the classics.

Posthumous Redaction?

Inglis's efforts to inform Latin pedagogy with progressive education theory were unlikely to appeal to factions at either extreme of the early twentieth-century debate over the place of the classics in the high school curriculum. In fact, evidence of the lack of appeal of Inglis's position appeared to surface in the posthumous completion and editorial handling of his last written work, an article published in *The Classical Journal*.[56] This article emerged from his work developing the English vocabulary test, discussed above.

At the time of his death in April 1924, six months after the publication of the description of the new English vocabulary tests, Inglis was in the early stages of what his Harvard colleagues, in their attempt to complete his unfinished work, called his "Language Project." According to a description of the project reconstructed by Harvard's Ralph W. Walter, Inglis's goal was to "provide materials for the study of language whereby an English Vocabulary may be acquired in the most complete, concise, and systematic manner."[57] From conversations with an Inglis associate and with Antoinette Inglis, Walter surmised that Inglis's project comprised five steps: extensive reading in the field of philology; a study of Latin derivatives in the English language; a study of prefixes and suffixes classified under origins; the design of instructional materials for high school teachers and students; and repetition of the same procedures for French, German, and Anglo-Saxon derivatives. Walter concluded, "We may even look forward to the day when the study of Latin, French, German, and English will be so coordinated in our high schools that the same vocabularies will be taught in each at the same point in the course. It was this very broad ideal that Professor Inglis had in mind." The correlation of the study of foreign language was, in fact, the topic of the seminar paper Inglis had prepared in 1908 while still a student at Teachers College, Columbia University.[58]

Although whether Inglis's colleagues saw his Language Project to fruition remains unclear, they did manage to submit Inglis's preliminary work for publication. Inglis's "Classical and Native Elements in the English Language" appeared posthumously in *The Classical Journal*.[59] Although the stated aim of this article was to determine the proportion of English vocabulary derived from Anglo-Saxon and classical words, it also included data for words of Scandinavian and "other" origins. The article presented an extensive review of previous studies of word origin, as well. These facts suggest that it represented the first two steps of Inglis's Language Project that Walter had reconstructed.

The article reported how Inglis had determined the origins of 10,161 words that Harvard's Godfrey Dewey found used in various frequencies in a "wide range" of written contexts, including newspapers, periodicals, works of fiction, correspondence, and advertising. This was the same material upon which Inglis had based the construction of his English vocabulary tests. Inglis categorized words by frequency of use: occurrences of more than 1,000, 101–1,000, 51–100, 11–50, 6–10, and 1–5. He tabulated the distribution of the 10,161 words across these categories in 100,056 word occurrences by language of origin. Inglis's findings demonstrated that the categories of higher frequency of use contained the fewest total occurrences and percentages of words of classical origin. His data revealed that the proportion of classical words increased as the frequency of word use decreased.[60] The concluding sentence of the article, however, stated the following:

> In conclusion it may be said that the Classical element plays a much larger part in English language than previous studies in this field indicate, and while this fact alone cannot be taken as sufficient justification for the study of Latin in the secondary school, the finding may serve to strengthen the position of Latin at a time when its place in the program of studies is being seriously questioned.[61]

Obviously, this conclusion contradicts the findings Inglis discussed in the article. But could it represent the change in his thinking to which Inglis alluded in his note to West? Let us examine this conclusion more closely.

First, as just noted, the conclusion is inconsistent with Inglis's discussion of his data. Although his data suggested that about 58 percent of the 10,161 words were of classical origin, Inglis did not discuss this figure. Instead, he drew attention to the positive relationship between greater frequency of use and Anglo-Saxon origin and the corresponding negative relationship between greater frequency of use and classical origin. Second, the conclusion is inconsistent with the goal of Inglis's larger "Language Project"—that goal having been to improve the learning of English vocabulary, not to justify the place of Latin in the school curriculum. Third, the conclusion in this article is notable for its dissimilarity with the lengthy discussions of the implications of data that characterized most of Inglis's previous scholarship. Fourth, this conclusion is notable for its inconsistency with his previous analyses of classical pedagogy and with his view of the place of Latin in the secondary school curriculum[62]; while in the past he presented all sides of such debates and, while not rejecting the classics, offered critical but constructive suggestions for the improvement of classical pedagogy, here Inglis appears simply to defend flatly the place of Latin in the curriculum. In short, the conclusion is so out of character with Inglis's work, that it is difficult to imagine him reaching it. How, then, can we explain this conclusion?

One possible explanation for this conclusion is that Inglis intended the sentence not as the conclusion of the article, but as the beginning of a discussion of the implications of his findings, a discussion he never completed. This possibility would have been more in character with his scholarly method. As noted, Inglis had completed neither the project nor even the manuscript. Archival records indicate that Bancroft Beatley, who was the best candidate for an Inglis protégé at Harvard, had Inglis's handwritten manuscript typed by the departmental secretary and then himself submitted it to *The Classical Journal.*[63] A second possible explanation, then, is that, in the process of preparing the unfinished manuscript for publication, Beatley added a concluding sentence. Insufficient evidence exists, however, to verify either of these possible explanations for the inconsistent concluding sentence that appeared in the published article.

A third possible explanation for the conclusion stems from unusual features of the published article. The article appears to have received more editorial input from *The Classical Journal* than was typical at the time: the editor added six footnotes to Inglis's article. The first note indicated that the piece represented Inglis's last study, emphasizing twice that he had "completed" it before he died. Archival documents, again, indicate that Inglis had completed neither the project nor even the manuscript. The other five notes pointed the reader to data about the proportion of classical derivatives in English; in four of these notes, the data qualifies or contradicts Inglis's claims. The remaining note indicates data that concurs with Inglis's finding that "[t]en different words account for more than one-fourth of all the word occurrences" that Inglis examined.[64] Let us examine the editor's four qualifying footnotes.

In the first instance, Inglis had identified George P. Marsh's work as the most commonly cited study of the proportion of Anglo-Saxon words in the English language. Inglis indicated that Marsh found an average of 83 percent of words of Anglo-Saxon origin in the writings of noted English authors, such as Chaucer, Shakespeare, Milton, and Swift. The editor's footnote, however, directed the reader to other analyses reported in an article by B. L. Ullman previously published in *The Classical Journal.* These analyses put Anglo-Saxon origins at 60 percent, 29.7 percent, and 27 percent.[65] In the second instance, Inglis had suggested that "attempts at sampling the English language as given in dictionaries would probably give very unreliable results, since contributions from the different languages of origin are very irregular within any alphabetic group and within other lexigraphic categories." The editor's note again directs the reader to figures reported in Ullman's article, which indicated that an analysis of 20,000 words in the Standard Dictionary found only 29.7 percent of words of Teutonic origin and 48.2 percent and 13 percent, respectively, of Latin and Greek origin. Ullman concluded, "we see that the figures indicate that the classical element, Latin and Greek, is over 100 percent larger than the Teutonic and that the Latin element alone is over 62 percent larger than the Teutonic."[66]

In the third instance, Inglis had cited recent studies of word origin other than Marsh's, including work by Eldridge and by Thorndike, but explained his choice of Dewey's examination of the problem because of its relatively greater comprehensiveness, accuracy, and availability. The editor's note again cited Ullman's article, which reported that in Thorndike's list of 10,011 words, 46.8 percent were of Latin origin. The note also referred to a figure reported in the report of The Classical Investigation, which put at 52 percent the proportion of the 17,303 words in Thorndike's extended list that were of Latin origin.[67] The editor's final footnote was added to Inglis's concluding sentence, qualifying or, in fact, validating the claim that, "In conclusion, it may be said that the Classical element plays a much larger part in English language than previous studies in this field indicate," with reference once more to Ullman's article. Ullman had concluded that the classical element in the English language was so pronounced that the "proper name for it [the English language] would be Latin-English, with Latin coming first."[68] Berthold L. Ullman, of the University of Iowa, served as an associate editor of *The Classical Journal.*

These editor's notes lend the article a tone of advocacy that was absent from and inconsistent with Inglis's recent work on classical pedagogy. Moreover, the editor's notes seem calculated to emphasize the role of Latin elements in the English language. After all, Inglis's finding that the proportion of classical derivatives in the English language decreased as the frequency of word use increased undermined a key argument for the place of Latin and Greek in the school curriculum. Indeed, the concluding sentence of Inglis's article seems better supported by evidence cited in the editor's notes than by Inglis's discussion of his data. A perusal of other volumes of *The Classical Journal* from the time period revealed Inglis's article as the only study to receive such substantive editorial input. The question of whether the inconsistent concluding sentence was the beginning of Inglis's discussion of the implications of the data, was added by Bancroft Beatley, or perhaps even was added by the editors of *The Classical Journal*, is almost rendered moot by the effect of the editor's footnotes. This not so subtle tactic for mitigating evidence viewed as a potential threat to the place of the classics in the curriculum reveals that, despite attempts such as Inglis's to apply progressive principles to Latin pedagogy, in the face of recent criticism of the value of the classics, corners of the classicist community struck a defensive posture.

Somewhat ironically, however, some of the recommendations of The Classical Investigation were closer to the kind of synthesis of classical pedagogy and progressive education theory and research that Inglis had called for in his 1922 *Classical Journal* article than was the closing sentence of the 1924 article. The Classical Investigation stands as the most extensive study of the teaching of Latin in secondary schools ever undertaken in the United States. In addition to contributions from dozens of classicists from around the country organized into regional committees, The Classical Investigation sought "the collaboration and criticism of forty-eight leading professors of education and psychology," most of whom were influential progressives. Additionally, twenty-nine additional education professors contributed "valuable advice and criticism" to sections of the report, among them Inglis, though the participation of these progressives, including Inglis, was minimal at best.[69]

The Classical Investigation recommended several practices that were consistent with proposals for Latin pedagogy that Inglis had earlier advanced. These included considering students' previous experience with language, tapping student interests for motivational purposes, and employing collateral readings about classical civilization in English.[70] In its discussion of classical pedagogy the report drew from numerous studies conducted by educationists for ways to improve Latin curriculum and instruction. The report concurred with the recommendations of the Committee on Classical Languages of the Commission on the Reorganization of Secondary Education for achieving transfer of learnings, quoting text from a committee report reproduced in Inglis's *Principles of Secondary Education* and citing that committee's position on the importance of the mastery of inflectional forms.[71] The report of The Classical Investigation also cited Inglis on role of the improvement of language as a vehicle for clarifying thinking.[72]

Despite these progressive style recommendations, however, The Classical Investigation maintained that the "indisputable primary immediate objective in the study of Latin is progressive development of the ability to read and understand Latin." Latin for the sake of Latin served as the prevailing value. Traditional practices, such as daily practice in sight reading, methods of reading instruction that only follow Latin (versus. English) word order, and drill—characterized by "almost perfect thoroughness and exactness" but, "whenever practicable," "functional and associative rather than merely mechanical in character"—would remain viable and essential features of the Latin classroom.[73] Of course, the sheer retention of Latin in the curriculum would necessitate the continuation of some traditional practices, practices that Latinists considered to have been perfected over centuries of experience. Moreover, The Classical Investigation recommended beginning the teaching of Latin two years earlier in the junior high school and stressed that it should continue through high school for a total of six years.[74]

The most significant recommendation in the General Report, however, was the call for emphasis on "functional Latin" and on "comprehension at sight." By functional Latin, the Advisory Committee meant the ability to apply formal rules of Latin within the language itself, that is, without first translating the Latin into English. Similarly, the exercise of comprehension at sight involved reading a Latin passage and responding to questions about its meaning, skipping the step of translating the passage into English. The emphasis on functional Latin and comprehension at sight represented a departure from conventional Latin pedagogy, which tended to emphasize understanding "formal" knowledge of Latin, that is, the rules, although the idea was not new.[75] In contrast to the progressive recommendations associated with Inglis, the emphasis on "functional Latin" in The Classical Investigation represented a relatively reactionary direction for Latin pedagogy to head in.

The Evolving High School

During the early 1920s, Inglis remained interested in wider problems of secondary education. The 7 November 1923 issue of *The New Republic* devoted a special section to consideration of "The American High School." In the lead article for this section, Inglis documented the numerical expansion of secondary school enrollments since 1890 as well as the corresponding expansion of the range of aptitudes and abilities of the student population. As he put it, "the clientele of the public secondary school has changed rapidly from a relatively homogeneous and select body to one which is very heterogeneous and representative of a wide range of social, economic, and intellectual status."[76] Inglis observed that the expansion of the high school curriculum and the diversification of the student population "reciprocally" affected each other, that is, the expansion of the curriculum attracted nontraditional students and the presence of nontraditional students resulted in the expansion of the curriculum. Inglis noted that, during the late nineteenth century, curriculum expansion occurred mainly among academic subjects and that during the opening decades of the twentieth century, curriculum expansion extended to vocational and commercial courses. Inglis argued, however, that curriculum expansion was a necessary but insufficient way to accommodate student needs. "A far more difficult problem faces us in the adaptation of secondary education to the varying capacities of pupils," he wrote.[77]

Historians have been wont to characterize progressive educators as believing that, as high school enrollments expanded during the twentieth century, most students lacked the intellectual capacity, that is, the IQ, to handle academic coursework, and as arguing that academic expectations for most students should be "dumbed down" through differentiated curriculum.[78] In the *New Republic* article Inglis continued, "The *academic* studies of our secondary school, *as at present ordinarily organized and taught*, require for successful accomplishment an intelligence probably not lower than five points above average ability," which meant to Inglis that "the academic studies of our high school are geared up so that they cannot be undertaken satisfactorily by more than one half of American citizens."[79] Was Inglis arguing that less able students should be exposed to less rigorous academic experiences? Does Inglis's position imply that not all students should have access to a rigorous academic subject matter? His language certainly leaves some room for such an interpretation. He continued, "It is perfectly possible for most American citizens to learn the limited amount of any high school study, provided it is organized and taught with proper regard for the capacities of the pupils concerned," wording that could well be interpreted to mean that some students should learn less academic subject matter than others. But in the same passage, Inglis also stated the following. Recognizing a historic and continuing selective function of secondary education, Inglis asked, "Can anyone hold that the selective factor should be such as to exclude more than one-half of our children from reasonably successful accomplishment in English, foreign languages, mathematics, science, and history?" Evoking an argument he had used to promote the improvement of classical pedagogy, Inglis continued, "It is not on record that the French language is reserved in France for those only who have an intelligence above the average." The implication of this argument is that, from Inglis's perspective, if French—and Latin—were taught properly, all American students should learn to speak them with everyday fluency—a goal that continues to elude foreign language educators. This held for other academic subjects, as well. Inglis called for "real adaptation of instruction to the varying capacities of the children concerned," a task that he considered "the most important and by far the most difficult problem to be faced in the field of secondary education."[80] For Inglis, the onus was the organization of curriculum and instruction to make subject matter accessible to students. Traditional academic formalism required transformation, and in effect, democratization, through the application of progressive principles of education. Inglis concluded by stating his opinion that "the conception that secondary education should exercise its selective function by differentiation rather than by exclusion, elimination, or failure, and that it should afford opportunities to each normally constituted citizen according to his capacities and needs" was "the only legitimate conception permissible in American society."[81]

Inglis also contributed a chapter about the American high school to a Festschrift for his former teacher Paul Monroe edited by I. L. Kandel, essentially an elaboration of his *New Republic* article.[82] Inglis discussed a half-dozen "significant phases of development" of the high school during the previous quarter century. The first of these phases involved increases both in enrollment and in the number of secondary schools in the United States, which, as he had discussed in the *New Republic* article, resulted in not only "the dominance of the public high school in the field of secondary education," but also in "a far more heterogeneous body in capacities, economic or social status, and educational needs than was the secondary school clientele of 1890 or 1900."[83] The second phase involved the expansion of programs and curricula beyond the academic to include commercial and vocational courses, as well as more "functional" variations of previously formalistic academic courses. Inglis identified five "new policies of curriculum organization" that emerged from this phase of development:

> (1) curricula based on as wide a variety of studies as is justified by the capacities and needs of the pupils concerned and the ability of the community to provide them, with proper regard for reasonable economy in support and for efficient instruction; (2) curricula in each of which adequate attention is paid to the proper balance of aims and functions in secondary education; (3) curricula so organized that as far as possible each pupil may secure the maximum of benefit according to the amount and character of his study, with due recognition of the fact that most pupils will not complete the full secondary course; (4) curricula organized with as much flexibility as possible so

> that necessary re-adjustments can be made by the pupil with a minimum of loss; (5) curriculum differentiation based on significant differences in the careers for which various groups of pupils are preparing themselves.[84]

The third phase involved securing an adequate number of well-educated teachers to serve the increased number of schools and pupils.

The fourth phase involved the emergence of new principles of instruction appropriate to the new student body. These principles included recognizing individual differences, less emphasis on academic formalism and more emphasis on "the functional in content and method," and greater emphasis on "social values in secondary education" through both selection of curriculum based on "social importance" and instruction that included "cooperative activity and the creation of classroom situations which as far as possible stimulate actual situations in life and provide social experience." These principles also included organizing subject matter not along the "scientific" view of the specialist, but instead "in terms of the laws of learning," less emphasis on the deferred value of a study and more on its immediate use to students, and greater emphasis on motivation of pupils. For Inglis, the implementation of these principles in secondary classrooms was far from complete. The fifth phase involved articulation of the secondary school with earlier levels of education, namely the emergence of the idea and practice of the junior high school as a transitional institution, and, less developed at the time of his writing, the emergence of "post-graduate" opportunities other than the four-year college, namely the junior college.[85]

The most important of the recent phases in the development of the high school, however, for Inglis involved changing conceptions of secondary education. Inglis asserted that "conceptions of the functions of secondary have changed from those dominated by selective ideals to those which postulate that the opportunities of secondary education should be made available for each citizen according to his needs, capacities, and willingness to make the necessary efforts."[86] Inglis noted that, historically, secondary education was "dominated by the conception that it is suitable and desirable for those only who, by virtue of social, economic, or intellectual superiority, can be expected to assume positions of leadership in life."[87] Recently, however, "people have ceased to look on it as an educational luxury to be reserved for the few."[88] Rather, "[d]evelopments of the past quarter-century have necessitated the substitution of selection by differentiation for the former selection by elimination and restricted instruction."[89] This is where Inglis had left off in the *New Republic* piece; he had also advanced this argument in *Principles of Secondary Education*. That is, secondary education dominated by academic formalism effectively kept the high school experience out of reach of all except those students who possessed a skill for academic work, a skill which, of course, was measured by the Intelligence Quotient. Academic formalism functioned to eliminate from school, and to limit educational opportunities for, students who were not academically oriented. Inglis argued that curriculum and instruction must be adapted to individual differences in order to accommodate the increasingly heterogeneous student population. This meant applying the progressive principles of instruction he had discussed earlier. "Secondary education," he concluded, "can never adequately perform its functions until subject matter and method are organized in terms of the varying capacities of pupils. This," he insisted, "is the most difficult, but probably the most important, problem to be solved."[90]

In summary then, from his assessment of the last quarter century of developments in and identification of future challenges facing the American high school, to his call for the application of progressive principles of teaching and learning to Latin instruction, his dissenting position on proposals to expand the role of the federal Bureau of Education, his work constructing intelligence quotient scales and achievement tests for English vocabulary and for Latin, and his responsibilities building the program in secondary education at the Harvard Graduate School of Education, during the early 1920s Inglis worked at the height of his ability and influence. Following his career as a Latin teacher, by his early forties, Inglis has successfully established for himself a career in higher education and had achieved influence and recognition as a leading progressive educator of his day. His work not only intersected but also transcended most of the interpretations historians have employed to explain early twentieth-century education, though he is probably most accurately characterized as a "pedagogical progressive." Inglis had identified the most important problems in secondary education to pursue and the environment at the new Harvard Graduate School of Education offered what were probably unparalleled conditions in which to pursue this work. Tragically, the opportunities to pursue this work would not be his.

CHAPTER SEVEN

The Inglis Legacy

On Wednesday, 9 April 1924, just having completed correspondence to a presidential search committee at his alma mater, Inglis experienced abdominal discomfort. Although the discomfort subsided temporarily, it returned the following day with severity sufficient enough to compel him to seek hospitalization. On Friday morning doctors performed emergency surgery and found an "intestinal abscess." According to Henry Holmes, a sac on Inglis's intestines "became infected and burst, giving him general peritonitis after an operation." On the morning of Saturday, 12 April 1924, Alexander Inglis, forty-four years of age, died, apparently of what the medical profession would later term diverticulitis. Inglis's funeral was held at 2:30 on the afternoon of Tuesday, 15 April 1924, at the South Congregational Church in Middletown, Connecticut. Nearly the entire Harvard Graduate School of Education faculty attended, with Henry Holmes and Walter Dearborn, as well as Frank W. Ballou, superintendent of the Washington, DC, public schools, serving as honorary bearers. His body was interred in a family plot adjacent to the graves of his mother, Susan Byers Inglis, and brother, Willie Inglis, on a westerly hillside in Indian Hill Cemetery.[1]

The Harvard Graduate School of Education community reeled in shock from Inglis's sudden and unexpected death. The immediate necessity of covering Inglis's classes was met by O. C. Gallagher, superintendent of the Brookline Schools, who taught Secondary School Administration and by Bancroft Beatley, who taught the rest. Holmes planned to cover Inglis's classes during the 1924–5 academic year by employing the services of a number of temporary and visiting instructors, including Guy Whipple, visiting from the University of Michigan, and Frank T. Spaulding.[2] Although Holmes had proposed to Lowell an external search for a junior faculty member, eventually Beatley and Spaulding assumed Inglis's duties in the Harvard Graduate School of Education.[3]

Over the weeks following Inglis's death, dozens of expressions of condolences arrived at the offices of the Harvard Graduate School of Education. Former students, colleagues, and educators with whom he had associated through his survey work and other activities contacted Holmes, among them George Counts, Leonard V. Koos, William Bagley, and James E. Russell. William H. Kilpatrick, for example, wrote, "American education is the poorer for the going of Professor Inglis. He has left a permanent impress for good. His work will live after him."[4] On 28 May 1924, the Harvard Graduate School of Education held a memorial service for Inglis. Five of his colleagues and students attested to his personal and professional qualities. From these remarks emerges a profile of Inglis as a thoughtful, enthusiastic, and personable teacher, as a frank but politic survey leader, and as an incisive and indefatigable scholar who possessed "an unlimited capacity for work" in every area of his responsibilities.[5] Henry Holmes claimed about Inglis, "He was among the pioneers in the systematic study of the problems of a great American institution, the secondary school." Referring to the Harvard Graduate School of Education, Holmes offered that Inglis's "reputation was an element of strength in the institution, perhaps the greatest it has had." Holmes continued, "In his work and in his association with his fellows, he 'played hard,' just as he did at football and baseball in his younger days." Holmes noted that in addition to his unfinished work in the area of testing, at the time of his death Inglis was also "writing on the theory of teaching and the administration of secondary schools."[6] The memorial closed with the singing of the Latin hymn, "Integer Vitae."

During the five months following Inglis's passing, his colleagues at the Harvard Graduate School of Education established the Inglis Lecture. Contributions from faculty, students, Harvard University overseers, and acquaintances of Inglis endowed the Inglis Memorial Lectureship Fund. Antoinette Inglis, over the objections of Henry Holmes, donated to the fund royalties from the Inglis Tests of English Vocabulary.[7] Within a year, a principal of $ 4,400 was considered sufficient to launch the annual lecture. In 1925, Leonard Koos delivered the first Inglis Lecture in secondary education. In introductory comments at the first lecture, Holmes said, "These lectures testify to the eminence he [Inglis] had achieved in his field . . . we felt the strong desire to continue his work, to contribute to the cause to which he was devoted."[8] The appendix to this book contains a list of the published Inglis Lectures. In 1937, the Wesleyan University class of 1902 founded the Al Inglis Scholarship Award, which Antoinette Inglis also supported.

Each year at Harvard as the lecture approached, Holmes sent Antoinette Inglis an invitation and a bouquet. After her husband's passing, Antoinette Clark Inglis left Cambridge to pursue a career as a painter. Her correspondence with Holmes indicates that over the years she lived variously in Manhattan, at Painters Farm in Chester Springs, Pennsylvania, in Boston, and in Annisquam, Massachusetts. Antoinette apparently attended some of the lectures. As each lecture was published, Holmes forwarded her a copy of the slim crimson volume. Once, she wrote to

Holmes, "The Inglis lecture set is one of my real treasures." On another occasion, she noted, "To be included in this memory means more and more to me as the years pass." By the 1940s, Antoinette had established a regional reputation as a painter, with exhibits of her work at galleries in Massachusetts and New York; she continued to paint through the 1960s. During the 1950s, Antoinette contributed an additional $ 2,000 to support the Inglis lecture; upon her death she bequeathed $ 5,000 to the lectures and $ 15,000 and all of the subsequent royalties of Alexander's books to support the secondary education programs at Harvard. Antoinette survived Alexander by nearly 49 years.[9]

Alexander Inglis had enjoyed a relatively brief but remarkable career. From his Latin pedagogy, to his historical study of the high school in Massachusetts, his systematic articulation of principles of secondary education, school survey work, and test development, not to mention his participation on the CRSE, work with the War Department, and his professional affiliations, Inglis traveled the prominent contours of the landscape of early twentieth century education in the United States. He was among the progressive educators who pioneered new conceptions of curriculum and instruction in response to changing circumstances in American education and culture.

Figure 7.1. Alexander James Inglis, probably 1921. Courtesy of Special Collections, Monroe C. Gutman Library, Harvard University Graduate School of Education.

What was Inglis's legacy? His Latin textbooks and intelligence scales remained in print and in use for decades, into the 1970s and 1960s, respectively, following his death. His historical study of the high school in Massachusetts remains a standard citation for education historians.[10] His *Principles of Secondary Education* initially was widely used and remained in print at least into the 1950s; Simmons claimed it eventually sold over fifty thousand copies. Authors of textbooks on secondary education frequently cited *Principles* on the history, aims, or organization of secondary education.[11] In 1955, about *Principles* Franzen contended,

> This book has had several successors, but none has ever equaled the job that he did. If it were not for certain complications that have prevented or stood in the way of a revision of the Inglis book so as to bring it up to date, it would still, in all probability, be the standard text in the field. At any rate, Inglis is the man who set the pattern for the content of the course for which his book was designed. The content is historical, philosophical, and sociological. It tells the whys and wherefores of the American secondary school system from its origins to its present-day status.[12]

Through his role on the CRSE Inglis impacted untold numbers of educators and students, helping to invent and promote a unique American educational institution that was implemented (to varying degrees) widely both in the United States and abroad, while his survey work often had a more immediate impact on education systems. The Inglis Lecture, merged in 1960 with the Burton Lecture, continues at the Harvard Graduate School of Education as the Inglis and Burton Lecture to provide a forum for the examination of issues of secondary education. In the long run, Inglis's greatest influence probably occurred through J. B. Conant, who drew heavily from *Principles* as he developed his conception of the comprehensive high school. Although Conant credited, among several educators, Francis T. Spaulding and Franklin J. Keller with having direct impact on his thinking about the American high school, it was Inglis's *Principles* from which he quoted generously in *The Child, the Parent, and the State.*[13]

Published the same year as Conant's influential study, *The American High School Today*, *The Child, the Parent, and the State* effectively articulated the extended rationale behind the famous work.[14] In fact, chapter four of *The Child, the Parent, and the State* Conant had first prepared for the 1959 Inglis Lecture. In this chapter Conant recounted the historical forces that, during the first three decades of the twentieth century, had transformed the public high school from an exclusive to an inclusive institution. Conant drew heavily from Inglis's *Principles,* quoting Inglis not only in the text of the chapters, but also in the endnotes; verbatim material from *Principles* comprised most of the more than five pages of endnotes. Conant spoke almost reverently of Inglis: "Reading Professor Inglis's volume in the light of what has happened since was to me a fascinating experience. One saw a revolution through the eyes of a revolutionary, one might almost say, or at least a reform through the eyes of a reformer." For Conant, the recommendations of Dewey, Inglis, and the CRSE "fit the new problems [faced by secondary schools] as a key fits a lock." Conant even suggested, "Professor Inglis was a member of the NEA Commission and, I judge, an influential member." Conant's faith in the comprehensive high school was such that he predicted that historians looking back from 2059 to the early twentieth century "will praise the revolutionary transformation of America's treatment of its children and of its youth" and will regard the resulting comprehensive high school model "not only as one of the finest products of democracy, but as a continuing insurance for the preservation of the vitality of a society of free men." Conant considered Inglis an "outstanding leader" of that development.[15]

At the time of his death, in addition to the language and testing projects discussed earlier, according to Henry Holmes, Inglis was at work on "a popular book dealing with the problems of the secondary-school teacher" and "had nearly completed another volume of his own on *Methods of Teaching in the Secondary School*."[16] Both of these manuscripts apparently perished, but their subject indicates that Inglis neither returned to Latin pedagogy nor abandoned his interest in teaching for wider policy issues. As noted above, at the Harvard Graduate School of Education memorial meeting for Inglis, Holmes mentioned that Inglis was "writing on the administration of secondary schools" as well. That in 1922 Inglis had responded to a student's query about what he thought to "be the greatest problem confronting education" with the reply, "[t]he reconstruction of the school curriculum," may indicate Inglis's future area of endeavor.[17] Given his evolving interests, variegated career, and impact, how is Inglis's career best understood?

Understanding Inglis's Career

Although the lack of pertinent source materials, such as a personal diary or interviews with his associates, prohibits anything approaching a definitive explanation of Inglis's motives and of the causes behind his actions—and prohibits the writing about Inglis of what Oakes calls a "pure biography"—a search for ways to understand Inglis's lifework can be rewarding. Let us first briefly situate Inglis's career in larger contexts of historical understanding of the progressive era and of the history of education research in the United States, and then explore the extent to which the four specialized historical interpretations mentioned at the outset apply to his work.

Born at the height of Victorian culture in America and working amidst the decline of that culture, Inglis's systematic and exhaustive scholarship seems to have manifested what historians have identified as Victorian values of hard work, conscientiousness, and even compulsion.[18] However much Inglis was imbued with these values, in his professional work he became the archetypal progressive reformer, exemplifying at least five definitive characteristics of the era. First, Inglis clearly fit the demographic profile of the progressive era reformer: white, "native-born, urban middle and upper middle class" professional endeavoring to resolve problems wrought by urbanization and industrialization. Second, Inglis's method bears a striking resemblance to the "distinctive method of progressive reform" that historians have reconstructed over decades of study of the period: thoroughly investigate a social problem, collect pertinent evidence, apply the modes of inquiry of the emerging social sciences to analyze that evidence, generate solutions that logically follow, work to implement the solution through a voluntary association.[19] Inglis's faith in the utility of new social sciences, another hallmark of progressivism, is particularly pronounced; from this perspective, *Principles of Secondary Education* stands as a quintessential statement of progressive values, as an attempt to generate organizing principles upon which to construct a new, responsive social institution.[20] His testing work manifests this faith as well.[21] Third, in addition to exhibiting the commitment of "reforming professionals" to "impartial expertise," Inglis, particularly in his survey work and in his position on the role of the federal government in education, manifested commitments to "direct democracy, community, and a form of government that was small yet responsive" that were typical of progressive reformers.[22] Fourth, Inglis's emphasis on promoting "social-cooperativeness" through the unifying function of the comprehensive high school reflects an "emphasis on social bonds and the social nature of human beings" characteristic of his era, though he, like most progressive reformers, stopped short of extending this ideal to African Americans.[23] Fifth, Inglis's commitment to social meliorism, rather than to revolution, reflects a liberal faith in progress also characteristic of progressive reformers.[24]

Historians of the progressive era discern in such reform efforts the broad effect of imposing middle-class values on society with a consequential expectation from reformers of recognition of their expertise and conferral of authority on them. Although Inglis clearly fits the profile of middle-class progressive reformers, and thus may well have harbored such expectations, such expectations on his part, other than his desire for promotion to the rank of professor, cannot be substantiated with available documentation. Additionally, historians maintain that the progressive reform impulse, in general and among education reformers, was "rooted in evangelical Protestantism."[25] Because surviving documentation offers no useful insight into Inglis's religious convictions or even practices, the role of religion in his lifework remains in question. Similarly, the historical riddle of what differentiated conservatives from progressives, which seems to apply to Inglis in his transformation from academic traditionalist to progressive experimentalist, stands unsolvable without additional documentation.[26] As noted, however, Inglis's inclination toward the pedagogical and not the philological or archeological sides of the classics probably predisposed him to pursue the new theory and science of progressive education. The pervasive conservatism among classicists could have contradicted Inglis's predilection for social meliorism, as well.

Inglis's case provides an opportunity to appreciate "the unexpected consequences of reform" that interests historians of the progressive era. McCormick indicated that many progressive reformers were unable to anticipate undesirable consequences of their endeavors and "were commonly surprised by the results of the reforms they so fervently sought." Inglis was able to anticipate consequences of some practices he promoted, but not of others. For example, as he advocated the junior high school as a gradual transition between elementary school and the senior high school, he cautioned that simply imposing the discipline-centered curriculum of the latter on the junior high school would undermine the intent of the junior high school. This in fact subsequently happened, prompting the middle-school movement during the late twentieth century. And, unlike most educators of his day, Inglis also somewhat presciently anticipated the politicization of the federal education agency as it achieved cabinet status.[27]

Although Inglis was able to anticipate such particularized consequences, he was unable, as were many, if not nearly all of his contemporaries, to anticipate more general consequences of progressive reforms. For example, while he advocated the use of standardized tests for the improvement of teaching and learning, he evidently did not foresee the emergence of the kind of system of meritocracy that Lemann traced from early testing efforts like Inglis's. Similarly, in his advocacy of universal secondary education, Inglis did not anticipate the emergence of the educational credentials market that Labaree chronicled. Of course, it would perhaps be expecting too much of any progressive reformer to foresee such complex and long-term consequences of their efforts. Distinctions between intentions and consequences of educational reforms warrant greater attention from educational and curriculum historians.[28]

Inglis's scholarship parallels the procession of methodologies that characterized the development of education research in the United States during the early twentieth century.[29] He navigated the main currents of contemporary education research, studying under Monroe and Thorndike at Teacher's College, Columbia University, conducting historical research, synthesizing sociological and psychological studies, accumulating knowledge of educational practice through his survey work, and constructing intelligence scales and achievement tests to yield more accurate information about student performance. Yet Inglis did not simply parrot his professors at Teachers College: although he was in accord with several of Thorndike's positions, he rejected Lodge and Sachs's commitment to the classics, Sachs and Monroe's approach to the secondary school, and Snedden's positions on the high school and on social efficiency. As noted, his history of secondary education in Massachusetts, particularly when viewed as of a piece with *Principles*, represents the progressive method of history, which endeavored "both to provide an account of how we came to the present moment of transition . . . and to connect this account to a program for future action."[30]

Moreover, Inglis's method of generating new principles of education together with his method of proposing improvements to local educational institutions through his survey work represent an application of tenets of American pragmatism in education. Childs's compelling analysis of the place of the philosophy of pragmatism in American culture and its manifestation in the work of progressive educators can be extended to Inglis. As suggested earlier, the pragmatic commitments to the method of science, to democracy, and to the reconstruction of traditional patterns of action in response to changing social conditions are evident in *Principles*, as well as in Inglis's survey work. Additionally, Inglis's calls to relate the school experience to the student's life in society, to engage students in purposeful activities, to tailor curriculum and instruction to the uniqueness of individual students, and to promote cooperative relations through school experiences are consistent with the practical implications of pragmatism for education that Childs identified in his overlooked study of pragmatic educators.[31] Childs offered a critical but constructive interpretation of progressivism in education that can serve as a useful alternative to the prevailing negative, even pessimistic historical interpretations of that movement.

Inglis's career can be understood in these general terms; in its particulars his career can illuminate our perspective on the progressive education movement of the early twentieth century. Let us examine the merits of several more specialized interpretations of his era for understanding Inglis's lifework. To what extent does Krug's social efficiency–social control thesis, Kliebard's status politics thesis, Cremin's revolution in secondary education thesis, and Tyack's category scheme of progressive educators explain Inglis's career?

Social Efficiency–Control Thesis

Inglis's career is perhaps too easily interpreted as a manifestation of an early twentieth century commitment to social efficiency–social control ideology.[32] Inglis, of course, participated in three developments considered by most historians to be virtually archetypal of that movement: Inglis served on the CRSE that prepared the infamous *Cardinal Principles* report; he contributed to or directed nine school surveys; he generated intelligence quotient scales and had begun developing standardized achievement tests. Moreover, Inglis frequently employed the language of efficiency, through use of terms such as *efficiency*, *social efficiency*, and even *social control* in his writing.

Yet, upon closer examination, important discrepancies exist between social efficiency–social control doctrine and Inglis's work. First, Inglis, frequently used the vocabulary of efficiency in a generic fashion to mean competence or effectiveness rather than narrow cost effectiveness.[33] Such usage appears in the *Cardinal Principles* report, as well.[34] As a watchword of early twentieth-century educational reform, the term "efficiency" was used as frequently and as casually as the term "restructuring" was used during the late twentieth century. Education and curriculum historians sometimes seem to have been content to flag the term without attending closely to its contextual usage, to assume face validity of the vocabulary without attempting to verify meaning through the context—or, from a postmodern perspective, to exalt the signifier over the signified.[35] Second, Inglis also sometimes designated meanings for the term efficiency that redefined even its contemporary connotations of cost effectiveness, as he did, for example, in his report to the Westchester County (NY) authorities.[36] And while the imposition of business values on public policy, and particularly on education policy and practice, was characteristic of the era, Inglis did not evoke business ideology in his proposals for educational reform.[37] When developing his principles of secondary education, Inglis drew support not from the doctrine of scientific management, but from research in the social and psychological sciences. Third, although Inglis was wedded to the new scientific, that is quantitative, approach to educational research and policy formulation, he was no slave to it. He candidly recognized the advantages and limitations of quantitative data.[38] Fourth, while Inglis clearly embraced the criterion of use or of utility in determining educational worth and aims, he did so in the name of improving educational quality and opportunity by providing educational experiences through which children and youth would learn not merely to recall, but to apply knowledge. Inglis sought not to narrow, but to broaden, educational opportunity. Fifth, even the tactic of identifying an educational development with social efficiency by associating it with a proponent of social efficiency (which Krug employed to categorize the *Cardinal Principles* report as such) fails with Inglis. Inglis, like Clarence Kingsley, was associated with Snedden, in Inglis's case as Snedden's student. (Charles Prosser was a classmate of Inglis's, as well, perhaps compounding such an association.) Yet Inglis's ideas about secondary education were, by and large, in opposition to Snedden's. Finally, the social efficiency–social control thesis fails to explain the first ten years of Inglis's career when, in effect, he professionally personified the precepts of the Committee of Ten report. Not only, then, does the social efficiency–social control thesis hold limited explanatory power for Inglis's work, but also in a number of important respects, his work contradicts that thesis.

Status Politics Thesis

The status politics thesis seems to offer limited explanatory power for Inglis's career, as well. That reformers sought status for their ideas appears self-evident. Inglis obviously sought status for his "treasured beliefs." But what motivation or purpose drove this search? The available evidence, largely in the form of his written work and his colleagues' assessment of him, suggests that Inglis's commitment was not merely to himself, but to something larger than himself. Through the most systematic study of the problems of the day, Inglis concluded that changing circumstances in society, pedagogical research and theory, and educational conditions warranted the systemic reform of secondary education. As one colleague put it, "Convictions, the result of careful analysis without prejudice or passion, were the only 'opinions' that ever carried weight with him or that he would ever deign to use himself."[39] Emerging from what Gaddis would term the "phase transition" of his doctoral studies, Inglis repudiated his earlier-held cherished commitments; he was all too willing to discard outmoded beliefs.[40] His advocacy of progressive principles of education was not about validating his beliefs, but was about improving the quality of secondary education. For Inglis, the struggle for status of educational ideas was not merely symbolic; it was a profoundly practical imperative. And because historians have documented that the desire to validate cherished beliefs "appealed not to the middle class in general but to troubled, usually marginal people who expressed inchoate anxieties in largely symbolic terms," the status politics thesis may have limited explanatory power in the area of curriculum history.[41] High profile advocates of curriculum reform, like Inglis, working in the mainstream of society hardly fit this characterization.

Revolution in Secondary Education Thesis

If social efficiency–social control and status politics interpretations seem to hold limited applicability to Inglis's lifework, the changes that Cremin described in his revolution in secondary education thesis are reflected in Inglis's career rather well. Inglis's early career manifested the conception of education presented in the Committee of Ten report; later in his career he contributed to and advocated the conception of education depicted in the *Cardinal Principles* report. Observations of acquaintances suggest that Inglis's transformation from academic traditionalist to progressive experimentalist was professionally and personally profound. For example, L. Thomas Hopkins, Inglis's student and later an influential progressive curricularist, remembered Inglis this way:

> My most intimate relationship at Harvard was with Alexander Inglis, professor of secondary education, a former Latin scholar who had reactivated his growth process into a new vision both of himself and of education. He was trying to atone for his past myopia by helping students broaden their perception of their opportunities and responsibilities as educators . . . he spent hours in private and in class considering how he was misled in the past and how he could contribute more to others in the future.[42]

A "revolution" in Inglis's thinking about secondary education that mirrored the "revolution in secondary education" that Cremin discerned is evident in Inglis's professional and scholarly activities. Initially through his doctoral studies and later in his research and writing, Inglis shifted his professional and intellectual allegiances from those initially invested in a conception of secondary education consistent with the proposals of the Committee of Ten to those tied to the "modern" conception of secondary education manifest in the *Cardinal Principles* report. As his thinking evolved, Inglis also contributed to the larger "revolution" through his writing, teaching, survey work, and participation on the CRSE. Professionally, Inglis personified Cremin's "revolution" thesis.

Inglis's work manifests Cremin's four characteristics of progressivism in education as well. For Cremin, progressivism in education meant "broadening the program and function of the school to include direct concern for health, vocation, and the quality of family and community life." Inglis proposed for secondary education wide-ranging social-civic, economic-vocational, and individualistic-avocational aims and to achieve them the comprehensive high school, which would be comprehensive in terms of both the students it served and the curriculum it offered. Progressivism in education also "meant applying in the classroom the pedagogical principles derived from new scientific research in psychology and the social sciences." Inglis employed the new science of education research to determine principles of secondary education. As a result, he rejected the theory of mental discipline as well as differences in intelligence based upon gender or race, and advocated the application of the new laws of learning to all classrooms, including and particularly Latin classrooms. Progressivism in education "meant tailoring instruction more and more to the different kinds of classes of children who were being brought within the purview of the school." Inglis advocated tailoring curriculum and instruction to the particular group and even to the individual student taught; he placed the onus for reaching the increasingly heterogeneous student population on curriculum and instruction, maintaining that application of the new laws of learning would make every subject, again, including Latin, accessible to all students. Finally, progressivism in education "implied a radical faith that culture could be democratized without being vulgarized, the faith that everyone could share not only in the benefits of the new science but in the pursuit of the arts as well." Inglis asserted that it was the special role of the school to foster aesthetic appreciations through experiences in literature, music, and design and related arts.[43] Cremin's interpretations of progressive education explain Inglis's career well.

Inglis and Pedagogical Progressives

Aspects of the agenda of administrative progressives appear in Inglis's survey work, but not to the degree that historians have documented it in the work of other educators, such as Ellwood Cubberley or Jesse Sears. For example, in the surveys in which Inglis recommended changes in governance of educational systems, notably for Virginia and Augusta, the stated aim was to depoliticize a system that demonstrably fostered political patronage at the expense of educational effectiveness.[44] When recommending such changes, Inglis appealed not to business ideology, but to political principle. For Inglis, bureaucratic organization should function not at the expense of, but in the interest of, local control over and continued improvement of educational quality and opportunity.[45]

An examination of the whole of Inglis's life's work, especially his school surveying and his later Latin pedagogy, reveals that he is better, though perhaps not completely, understood as a "pedagogical progressive" rather than as an "administrative progressive." This is especially evident in his last works, in which he argued again that the greatest implication of changing social circumstances, particularly those that led to an increasingly heterogeneous student population, was the need "to adapt instruction to the varying capacities of those whom we encourage to attend the high school."[46] Yet because Inglis viewed such accommodation of individual needs as a means for undermining academic formalism and thereby for making subject matter increasingly accessible to students, he does not completely fit Tyack's characterization of pedagogical progressives as devoted to "subverting the hegemony of established school subjects."[47] The categorical disdain that recent historians have claimed progressives held for subject matter is not evident in Inglis's work.[48] Although Inglis would reduce the amount of academic work that was remote from students' needs, he also argued that academic subject matter had its place, especially if not taught in a formalistic fashion. Inglis contended, for example, that, although because of its limited utility all students should not study Latin, nevertheless the application of progressive principles of learning should enable all students to learn Latin.[49]

Inglis's work was pioneering in the synthesis of contemporary educational theory and research that he achieved. *Principles of Secondary Education* was, after all, the first grand synthesis of theory and research about secondary education. Through this synthesis, Inglis was able to arrive at conclusions that were pioneering for his day. His proposals also sought synthesis of aspects of educational practice that are often pitted against one another. He endorsed the consolidation of academic and vocational education in the comprehensive high school. He advocated the unification of students from all walks of life in the comprehensive high school. He championed the synthesis of traditional academic subject matter and progressive principles of pedagogy. He promoted a synthesis of the nature of the student, the subject matter, and the society as complementary considerations in selecting educational purposes and curriculum content; by not aggrandizing the importance of any one of these three sources, as other educators were wont to do, his educational theory transcended and perhaps held potential even to resolve theoretical disputes of the day.

Toward a Nuanced, Usable Curriculum History

The historical interpretations of education in early twentieth-century United States discussed above manifest varying degrees of explanatory power when applied to Inglis's career. At the same time, in some respects, aspects of Inglis's career contradict these interpretations. As an interpretation illuminates some dimensions of his career, it eclipses others. Inglis's work at once embodies complexities within and complicates broad interpretations of progressivism in education. Similarly, although Kliebard, Powell, and Tanner and Tanner's assessments of Inglis each contain an element of truth, in each case evoked in support of the development of a general interpretation, these assessments capture the whole truth, so to speak, neither of Inglis's career nor of the period during which he worked. Kliebard's characterization of *Principles* as a work of individual genius that stands apart from the *Cardinal Principles* report is problematic because Inglis contributed to the development of that report and because the ideas he articulated in his book are virtually identical to the major proposals offered by the commission. Powell's characterization of Inglis's work as an unimaginative reflection of contemporary emphasis on the social functions of education oversimplifies Inglis's comprehensive theory of secondary education, which actually sought a synthesis of the nature of society, the student, and the subject matter in the selection of educational purposes and curriculum content. Tanner and Tanner's recognition of Inglis's advocacy of the comprehensive high school and his consideration of three sources of curriculum purposes and content, nevertheless focuses too narrowly on that point in his career, neglecting Inglis's other important contributions.[50]

In the process of providing an overall sense of an age, or even an overall sense of an individual's lifework, general interpretations tend to simplify the sheer complexity of the past. Telling nuances are often lost. Of course, no particular historical interpretation is expected actually to grasp the definitive truth of any era. Consensual interpretations, however, often assume the status of metanarrative, distracting attention from alternative interpretations and even from contradictory evidence.

Biography, however, with its attention to the quality of detail in individual lives, can enhance appreciation of the sheer complexity of the past. Depaepe, for example, suggests, "Biography provides a welcome supplement to the abstract void that the structuralist, leftist-revisionist and neo-Marxist explanatory schemata have neglected." He continues, "In an educational *histoire totale*, narrative material is essential for supplementing, nuancing, and correcting circumstantial and coarse-grained normalization theories."[51] Educational biography can complement general period interpretations by reconstructing finer-grained representations of our educational past. And when "pure biography" is not feasible, as in Inglis's case, a lifework history can illuminate details of a period obfuscated by general interpretations. Yet although the anomalous nuances that emerge from a close examination of Inglis's work are provocative, they are probably insufficient by themselves to warrant substantive revision of accepted historical interpretations. Additional detailed reconstructions of educational careers from the period are in order. Perhaps eventually a prosopography, that is, a "collective biography," will yield a higher resolution composite profile of early twentieth-century education than heretofore possible through grainy general interpretations.[52]

Meanwhile, the work of educators who fit Tyack's profile of pedagogical progressives, such as Inglis's, has not been given its due—at best, historians merely highlight disputes between child-centered and subject-centered pedagogical progressives. Instead, educational and curriculum historians have consistently paid greater attention to the work of administrative progressives on the grounds that they enjoyed a greater practical impact on American education than did the pedagogical progressives. This is a valid reason, although the extent of the impact of the administrative progressives may have less to do with the force of their ideas than with the relative logistical ease of influencing the organization and structure of educational bureaucracies, compared to the complexity of influencing the content and nature of pedagogy.[53]

The neglect of pedagogical progressives is problematic for at least two reasons. First, as just suggested, the prevailing interpretations have distracted historians and educators seeking to learn from history from inconsistencies and anomalies in the historic record that contradict and are not explainable by these interpretations. Inglis's early rejection of any relationship between race and intelligence, his unorthodox conception of "efficiency," and his efforts to synthesize traditional academic values and progressive educational science stand as notable examples of such anomalies. Second, the neglect of pedagogical progressives not only leaves our educational and curriculum history incomplete, but also makes our educational and curriculum past less "usable," to borrow Van Wyck Brooks's term, than it perhaps can be.[54] Unlike educational historians, who are committed to approaching the historic record largely as a text to analyze and explain for academic ends, curriculum historians tend to approach the historic record also as a repository of professional thought and practice.

From the perspective of curriculum history, we can potentially learn not only from past mistakes, but also from past successes, upon which we hopefully can build. The focus on the administrative progressives not only harps on past mistakes, perhaps even implying that there is little to salvage from the lost endeavors of our professional predecessors, but also obscures past successes that may still hold practical relevance in the present. Rather than continue to turn a blind eye toward pedagogical progressives, it is time to recover the constructive legacy that they left through a high definition representation of their work. The endeavors of previously ignored progressive educators like Inglis, Junius Meriam, Frederick Bonser, Thomas Briggs, Leonard Koos—to name a few—warrant close attention. Given, for example, late nineteenth- and early twentieth-century high school and college curricula, the likelihood is great that other progressive educators were immersed in the classics during their formative years, though few pursued the subject to the extent that Inglis did. What led these educators away from traditional academic education toward progressive ideas and practices? If Inglis's career is any indication, we have much not only of historical, but also of practical value to learn from our predecessors.

Now that we have considered how a reconstruction of Inglis's lifework can possibly inform our understanding of the educational past, a brief consideration of ways that Inglis's work can inform the educational present seems in order. What principles and practices advocated by Inglis hold relevance for education practice during the early twenty-first century? No doubt, many aspects of Inglis's work, from his articulation of aims of secondary education, to his analysis of subject values, to his proposal to organize the secondary curriculum into constants, special curriculums, and free electives, and even to his translation of Cicero's *Essay on Friendship*, may interest educators. In addition to the perhaps overly optimistic hope that proposals for education reform emerge from the kind of systematic review of research, theory, and practice in which Inglis engaged, at least the following aspects of his work seem to speak to present conditions.

The current preoccupation with academic achievement could be informed by two of Inglis's recommendations. One is his contention that academic subject matter can be made accessible by implementing classroom practices that overcome the severe limitations of academic formalism, which, for Inglis, was too often mistaken for academic rigor. For Inglis, employment of research-based techniques that, for example, relate new material to previous learning, motivate students, and provide opportunities for the application of subject matter, would make even esoteric subjects like Latin accessible to all students. Another is Inglis's frank recognition of the limitations of standardized testing. The often cynical blind faith that some school reform advocates place in standardized testing flies in the face of decades of established psychometric theory and practice; the misuse of such tests will likely result in miseducation. Inglis's understanding, in effect, that standardized tests were potentially helpful, but imperfect instruments, remains relevant.

In an age in which the heterogeneity of American society continues to increase and in which economic policy has widened disparities in income and wealth and sharpened social class divisions, the unifying function of the comprehensive high school that Inglis advocated assumes special relevance. He argued,

> As an efficient social institution secondary education must recognize the necessity of provision for training which shall serve to make for integration, training which shall allow for the individual differences among pupils and the differentiated needs of society, training in which the supplementary relation of the two factors is observed.[55]

For Inglis, the "increasing complexity of life in a modern democracy constantly increases the amount of common knowledge, of common action, and common ideals necessary." He argued that "increasing heterogeneity of the population" and "increasing diversity of industrial occupations" combined with "problems of 'class distinction'" made attention to the integrating or unifying function of secondary education imperative.[56] From his recognition of the reality of the need for both unification of and specialization within society to his recommendations for promoting democratic cooperation through the operations of the school, Inglis offered an alternative to social and educational fragmentation that increasingly characterizes the United States in the early twenty-first century—recognizing, of course, that the unifying function of secondary education today would be far more inclusive than in his day.

Given the developments in education research that have occurred since Inglis's time, recognition of the currency of these or any aspects of his work in our time would represent just the beginning of a process that would include not only an analysis of the local situation, but also a systematic review of relevant theory, research, and practice that pertained to the particular principle Inglis endorsed. Indeed, from Inglis's survey work we can appreciate the practical imperative of diagnosing actual educational conditions as a precursor to prescribing improvements appropriate to the local circumstances; from his development of principles of secondary education we can appreciate the value of systematic review of theory, research, and practice. Perhaps Inglis's consummate method of resolving educational problems is the most pragmatic and important legacy that he left.

Appendix: The Inglis Lectures

1925 Leonard Koos. *Trends in American Secondary Education.*
1926 Paul Hanus. *Opportunity and Accomplishment in Secondary Education.*
1927 Abraham Flexner. *Do Americans Really Value Education?*
1928 Charles H. Judd. *The Unique Character of American Secondary Education.*
1929 George S. Counts. *Secondary Education and Industrialism.*
1930 Thomas H. Briggs. *The Great Investment.*
1931 John Dewey. *The Way Out of Educational Confusion.*
1932 William S. Learned. *Realism in American Education.*
1933 Henry C. Morrison. *The Evolving Common School.*
1934 I. L. Kandel. *The Dilemma of Democracy.*
1935 Samuel S. Drury. *The Care of the Pupil.*
1936 John L. Tildsley. *The Mounting Waste of the American Secondary School.*
1937 Edward L. Thorndike. *The Teaching of Controversial Subjects.*
1938 Malcolm S. MacLean. *Scholars, Workers, and Gentlemen.*
1939 Charles A. Prosser. *Secondary Education and Life.*
1940 Aubrey. W. Williams. *Work, Wages, and Education.*
1941 Mark A. May. *Education in a World of Fear.*
1942 Floyd W. Reeves. *Education for Today and Tomorrow.*
1943 Paul R. Mort. *Secondary Education as Public Policy.*
1944 George D. Stoddard. *Tertiary Education.*
1945 G. F. Zook. *The Role of the Federal Government in Education.*
1946 Mark Starr. *Labor Looks at Education.*
1947 Ordway Tead. *Equalizing Educational Opportunities Beyond the Secondary School.*
1948 Allison Davis. *Social-Class Influences Upon Learning.*
1949 Harold Benjamin. *The Cultivation of Idiosyncrasy.*

1950 Margaret Mead. *The School in American Culture.*

1951 Julius Seelye Bixler. *Education for Adversity.*

1952 Theodore M. Green. *Liberal Education Reconsidered.*

1953 Willard B. Spaulding. *The Superintendency of Public Schools—An Anxious Profession.*

1954 Henry Lee Smith. *Linguistic Science and the Teaching of English.*

1955 Henry Wyman Holmes. *"... the last best hope...": Democracy Makes New Demands on Education.*

1956 Vera Micheles Dean. *The American Student and the Non-Western World.*

1957 Horace Mann Bond. *The Search for Talent.*

1958 Max Beberman. *An Emerging Program of Secondary School Mathematics.*

1959 James Bryant Conant. *The Revolutionary Transformation of the American High School.*

Notes

Introduction

1. Alexander James Inglis, *Principles of Secondary Education* (Boston: Houghton Mifflin, 1918); William Marshall French, *American Secondary Education*, 2nd ed. (NY: Odyssey Press, 1967), 142.
2. Commission on the Reorganization of Secondary Education, *Cardinal Principles of Secondary Education,* Bulletin 1918, No. 35, Department of the Interior, Bureau of Education (Washington, DC: U.S. Government Printing Office, 1918).
3. Herbert M. Kliebard, "The Curriculum Field in Retrospect," in *Technology and the Curriculum*, ed. Paul Witt (NY: Teachers College Press, 1968), 69–84; Arthur G. Powell, *The Uncertain Profession: Harvard and the Search for Educational Authority* (Cambridge, MA: Harvard University Press, 1980), 112–14; Daniel Tanner and Laurel Tanner, *History of the School Curriculum* (NY: Macmillan, 1990), 363–4.
4. Brief bios include Frank E. Spaulding, "Inglis, Alexander James," *Dictionary of American Biography*, vol. 9 (NY: Charles Scribner's Sons, 1932), 475–6; "Inglis, Alexander James," *The National Cyclopaedia of American Biography*, vol. 23 (NY: James T. White, 1933), 54; Robert Emans, "Inglis, Alexander James," in *Biographical Dictionary of American Education*, ed. John F. Ohles (Westport, CT: Greenwood, 1978), 692–3.
5. Stephen B. Oates, ed., *Biography as High Adventure: Life-Writers Speak on Their Art* (Amherst, MA: University of Massachusetts Press, 1986), ix–x. See also Craig Kridel, ed., *Writing Educational Biography: Explorations in Qualitative Research* (NY: Garland, 1998); Kathleen Cruikshank, "Educational History and the Art of Biography," review essay of *And There Were Giants in the Land* by John A. Beineke, *American Journal of Education* (May 1999): 231–9.

6. Lawrence A. Cremin, "The Revolution in American Secondary Education, 1893–1918," *Teachers College Record* 56 (March 1955): 295.
7. Ibid., 307.
8. Edward A. Krug, *The Shaping of the American High School, 1880–1920* (Madison, WI: University of Wisconsin Press, 1969), 249–50.
9. David B. Tyack, *The One Best System: A History of American Urban Education* (Cambridge, MA: Harvard University Press, 1974), 196.
10. Ibid., 197.
11. See, for example, Krug, *Shaping of the American High School*, 318ff; David L. Angus and Jeffrey E. Mirel, *The Failed Promise of the American High School, 1890–1995* (NY: Teachers College Press, 1999), 32ff; see also Michael W. Apple, *Ideology and Curriculum*, 2nd ed. (NY: Routledge, 1990), 75ff.
12. Herbert M. Kliebard, *The Struggle for the American Curriculum, 1893–1958*, 3rd ed. (NY: RoutledgeFalmer, 2004), xv.
13. Ibid., 289.
14. Ibid., 290.

Chapter One

1. See Arthur Raymond Mead, *The Development of Free Schools in the United States*, Contributions to Education No. 91 (NY: Teachers College, Columbia University, 1918); Emit Duncan Grizzell, *Origin and Development of the High School in New England Before 1865* (NY: Macmillan, 1923), 195–201; Orwin Bradford Griffin, *The Evolution of the Connecticut State School System*, Contributions to Education No. 293 (NY: Teachers College, Columbia University, 1928), 101–117.
2. H. F. Donlan, *The Middletown Tribune Souvenir Edition* (Middletown, CT: E.F. Bigelow, 1896), 10–11. Middlesex County (CT) Historical Society. This building ceased to serve as a school in 1972; in 1978 it was converted to a retirement home. See Elizabeth A. Warren, *A Pictorial History of Middletown* (Norfolk, VA: Dannings, 1990), 76.
3. *Report of the Dedicatory Exercises at the Opening of the New High School of the Middletown City School District, March 26th, 1896* (Middletown, CT: Pelton & King, 1896), 18, Middlesex County (CT) Historical Society.
4. William North Rice, "The High School and Its Relationship to Other Educational Institutions," *Report of the Dedicatory Exercises at the Opening of the New High School of the Middletown City School District, March 26th,*

1896 (Middletown, CT: Pelton & King, 1896), 25, Middlesex County (CT) Historical Society.

5. Ibid., 26, 27, 31.
6. "Died in Newark," *The Penny Press*, Wednesday, 6 January 1892, 3. One year later, Willie's remains were moved to the Indian Hills Cemetery in Middletown. Obituaries for Susan Beyer and William Grey Inglis appeared in *The Penny Press*, 19 November 1914, 10, and *Middletown Press*, 19 June 1939, 5, Russell Library, Middletown, CT. Dean Acheson, "My Morning in America," *Saturday Evening Post*, 15 December 1962, 27–9.
7. National Center for Education Statistics, *Digest of Education Statistics 2002* (Washington, DC: U.S. Government Printing Office, 2003), 69, 127.
8. Krug, *Shaping of the American High School, 1880–1920*, 11. See also Theodore R. Sizer, *Secondary Schools at the Turn of the Century* (New Haven, CT: Yale University Press, 1964); William J. Reese, *The Origins of the American High School* (New Haven, CT: Yale University Press, 1995); Jurgen Herbst, *The Once and Future School: Three Hundred and Fifty Years of American Secondary Education* (NY: Routledge, 1996).
9. National Education Association, *Report of the Committee of Ten on Secondary School Studies, Education Report, 1892–93* (Washington, DC: U.S. Government Printing Office, 1893), 1444. See Sizer, *Secondary Schools at the Turn of the Century.*
10. Caroline Winterer, *The Culture of Classicism: Ancient Greece and Rome in American Intellectual Life* (Baltimore, MD: The Johns Hopkins University Press, 2002), 1. For an analysis of Latin in wider contexts, see Francoise Waquet, *Latin or the Empire of a Sign: From the Sixteenth to the Twentieth Centuries* (London: Verso, 2001).
11. Winterer, *Culture of Classicism*, 156, 175.
12. National Education Association, *Report of the Committee of Ten*; American Philological Association, "Report of the Committee of Twelve on Courses of Study in Latin and Greek for Secondary Schools," *Transactions and Proceedings* 30 (1899): xxix–cxxi; Ken F. Kitchell, "The Great Latin Debate: The Futility of Utility?" in *Latin for the 21st Century: From Concept to Classroom*, ed. Richard A. LaFleur (Glenview, IL: Scott Foresman-Addison-Wesley, 1998), 11; Krug, *Shaping of the American High School*, 83.
13. Murray George Walter, "Development of the Public High School in Middletown, Connecticut, during the Years from 1840 to 1890"

(Masters thesis, Teachers College, Columbia University, 1932), photocopy at Middlesex County (CT) Historical Society.

14. *Forty-First Annual Report of the Board of Education of the Middletown City School District, September 1, 1898* (Middletown, CT: Pelton & King 1898), 23, Russell Library, Middletown, CT.
15. *Fortieth Annual Report of the Board of Education of the Middletown City School District, September 1, 1897* (Middletown, CT: Pelton & King, 1897), 25, Russell Library, Middletown, CT.
16. *Report of the Committee of Ten*, 1424; American Philological Association, "Report of the Committee of Twelve," xcvii–xcviii, cx.
17. *Forty-First Annual Report of the Board of Education of the Middletown City School District, September 1, 1898* (Middletown, CT: Pelton & King, 1898), 28, 33, Russell Library, Middletown, CT.
18. "Graduating Exercises," *The Penny Press*, Friday, 24 June 1898, Middlesex County (CT) Historical Society.
19. *Catalogue of Wesleyan University, 1898–99* (Middleton, CT, 1898), 27–30, Special Collections and Archives, Olin Library, Wesleyan University.
20. Academic Transcript for Alexander James Inglis, Office of the Registrar, Wesleyan University, obtained with the permission of his nephew Mr. David M. Brooks of Bedford, NH.
21. David B. Potts, *Wesleyan University, 1831–1910: Collegiate Enterprise in New England* (New Haven, CT: Yale University Press, 1992), 118, 146.
22. Ibid., 183, 186.
23. *The Olla Podrida* (1903), 31, *The Wesleyan Argus*, 35, no. 29, 29 June 1902, 255, Special Collections and Archives, Olin Library, Wesleyan University. Henry W. Holmes, "Minute on the Life and Services of Professor Alexander James Inglis," typed manuscript, collection of author.
24. See Frederick Rudolph, *The American College and University: A History* (NY: Vintage, 1962), 272, 334; John R. Thelen, *A History of American Higher Education* (Baltimore, MD: Johns Hopkins University Press, 2004), chaps 4 and 5. Sources for Inglis's course work in this and the following paragraph are Academic Transcript for Alexander James Inglis, Office of the Registrar, Wesleyan University, obtained with the permission of his nephew Mr. David M. Brooks of Bedford, NH; *Catalogue of Wesleyan University, 1898–99* (Middletown, CT, 1898); *Catalogue of Wesleyan University, 1899–1900* (Middletown, CT, 1899); *Annual Catalogue of Wesleyan University, 1900–01* (Middletown,

CT: Pelton & King, 1900); *Catalogue of Wesleyan University, 1901–2* (Middletown, CT, 1901), Special Collections and Archives, Olin Library, Wesleyan University.

25. Scrap Book—Exam Questions, Special Collections and Archives, Olin Library, Wesleyan University.
26. *The Olla Podrida* (1901), 214, Special Collections and Archives, Olin Library, Wesleyan University.
27. *The Olla Podrida* (1902), 199, Special Collections and Archives, Olin Library, Wesleyan University.
28. *The Olla Podrida* (1903), 31, Special Collections and Archives, Olin Library, Wesleyan University. Officer's Records, Horace Mann School, Columbia University, vol. 6, RG1 790005, Special Collections, Milbank Memorial Library, Teachers College, Columbia University.
29. *Kiskiminetas School Catalog*, 1901–2, *Kiskiminetas School Catalog*, 1902–3, *The Kiskiminetan*, 24 April 1903, *The Kiskiminetan*, 22 May 1903, Lawrence Nanney and Barbara Nanney, *Kiski: The First 100 Years* (Saltsburg, PA: The Kiski School, 1988), Alumni Office, the Kiski School.
30. Lawrence A. Cremin, David A. Shannon, and Mary Evelyn Townsend, *A History of Teachers College, Columbia University* (NY: Columbia University Press, 1954), 102.
31. Alexander James Inglis, *Key to Pearson's Latin Prose Composition* (NY: American Book Company, 1904); Alexander James Inglis and Virgil Prettyman, *First Book in Latin* (NY: Macmillan, 1906); Charles McCoy Baker and Alexander James Inglis, *High School Course in Latin Composition* (NY: Macmillan, 1909). Although Inglis's time at the American School of Classical Studies is noted in files of institutions where he worked, including the Horace Mann School and Harvard University, an inquiry to the American School of Classical Studies could not verity his formal enrollment there, as no records were maintained of summer visitors, personal communication, 11 September 2006.
32. *Bulletin of the Horace Mann Schools* (NY: Teachers College, Columbia University, 1907–8), 31; *Bulletin of the Horace Mann Schools* (NY: Teachers College, Columbia University, 1909–10), 32–3, Special Collections, Milbank Memorial Library, Teachers College, Columbia University.
33. Lee Byrne, review of *First Book in Latin*, by Alexander Inglis and Virgil Prettyman, *The Classical Journal* 4 (November 1980): 45.
34. Baker and Inglis, *High School Course*, vii.

35. Marcus Tullius Cicero, *Essay on Friendship (Laelius De Amicitia)* trans. with notes Alexander J. Inglis (NY: Newton and Cartwright, 1908). Platt and Peck Publishers issued a volume with identical text, save for the omission of a frontispiece portrait of Cicero, in a deluxe edition.
36. Ibid., v–vi.
37. Anthony Grafton, *The Footnote: A Curious History* (Cambridge, MA: Harvard University Press, 1997), 108. Grafton explains that the practice apparently is connected with "the authority long enjoyed by German philology in America, and lays particular weight on the habit of citing Ulrich von Wilamowitz-Mollendorff, the student of Greek literature and religion whose editions and analyses of texts remain deeply influential decades after his death" (p. 108).
38. *Bulletin of the Horace Mann Schools* (NY: Teachers College, Columbia University, 1906–7), 35, Special Collections, Milbank Memorial Library, Teachers College, Columbia University.
39. Walter Carter, notes for *All the Rage: Mandolin Ensemble Music from 1879–1924* (NY: New World Records, 1998), 8.
40. John F. Ohles, ed., *Biographical Dictionary of American Educators*, vol. 3 (Westport, CT: Greenwood, 1978), 806; Walter R. Agard, "Classical Scholarship," in *American Scholarship in the Twentieth Century*, ed. Merle Curti (Cambridge, MA: Harvard University Press, 1953), 148–9; William M. Calder, III, "Classical Scholarship in the United States: An Introductory Essay," in *Biographical Dictionary of North American Classicists*, ed. Ward W. Briggs, Jr (Westport, CT: Greenwood, 1994), xxviii; Winterer, *Culture of Classicism*, 173.
41. Inglis's course taking at Teachers College was reconstructed by matching his incomplete student records with published college announcements. His transcripts were obtained from the Teachers College Office of the Registrar with the permission of his nephew Mr. David M. Brooks of Bedford, NH. Course descriptions and instructors are recorded in the *Teachers College Announcement* for 1907–8 and 1909–10, Special Collections, Milbank Memorial Library, Teachers College, Columbia University.
42. Dumas Malone, ed., *Dictionary of American Biography*, vol. 16 (NY: Charles Scribner's, 1935), 280–1; Ohles, *Biographical Dictionary of American Educators* vol. 3, 1138; "Departmental Notes," *Teachers College Record* 3 (January 1902): 37–8.
43. Alexander J. Inglis, "Co-Operation and Correlation in Language Teaching in the High School," *Teachers College Record* 10 (March 1909): 63.

44. These volumes remained in the family, first with Antoinette Inglis, Alexander's widow, and then with David M. Brooks, Inglis's nephew. Currently, they are deposited at Special Collections and Archives, Olin Library, Wesleyan University.

Chapter Two

1. For a profile of the intellectual climate at Teachers College during the opening decades of the twentieth century, see Cremin, Shannon, and Townsend, *A History of Teachers College*, 41–58.
2. John Lewis Gaddis, *The Landscape of History: How Historians Map the Past* (Oxford: Oxford University Press, 2002), 120.
3. Cremin, "The Revolution in American Secondary Education, 1893–1918."
4. Alexander James Inglis, "Teachers' Pension Systems in the United States: An Analysis and Criticism" (M.A. thesis, Faculty of Philosophy, Columbia University, 17 April 1909), Special Collections, Milbank Memorial Library, Teachers College, Columbia University.
5. Documentation of his dissertation committee appears on the index card recording the bibliographical information of the publication of his dissertation as Teachers College Contributions to Education, No. 45, Office of the Registrar, Teachers College.
6. Alexander James Inglis, *The Rise of the High School in Massachusetts*, Teachers College Contributions to Education, No. 45 (NY: Teachers College, 1911).
7. Ibid., 30, 67.
8. Ibid., 105.
9. Ibid., 104.
10. See Milton Gaither, *American Educational History Revisited: A Critique of Progress* (NY: Teachers College, 2003), 97–9.
11. Inglis, *Rise of the High School in Massachusetts*, 160.
12. Officers Records, Horace Mann School, vol. 6, RG1 790005, Special Collections, Milbank Memorial Library, Teachers College, Columbia University.
13. "Belmont School," *San Mateo Times Gazette*, 1 August 1885; 19 December 1885; Ria E. Dewing, *Heritage of the Wooded Hills: Belmont History* (Belmont, CA: Belmont Historical Society, 1977), 29–32.
14. See "Inglis, Antoinette Clark," *Who's Who of American Women* (Chicago: Marquis, 1959), 632; "Matrimonial Announcement," *Cortland (NY)*

Standard, December 1911, and biographical card for William Heermans Clark, Cortland Historical Society, Cortland, NY.

15. *The Cricket*, December 1911, 12, 13, 18, *The Cricket*, May 1912, 51, 52, Belmont Historical Society, Belmont, CA.
16. Tyack, *The One Best System*; David Tyack and Elisabeth Hansot, *Managers of Virtue: Public School Leadership in America, 1820–1980* (NY: Basic Books, 1982); Kliebard, *The Struggle for the American Curriculum, 1893–1958*; Herbert M. Kliebard, *Schooled to Work: Vocationalism and the American Curriculum, 1876–1946* (NY: Teachers College, 1999); Diane Ravitch, *Left Back: A Century of Failed School Reforms* (NY: Basic Books, 2000).
17. Alexander J. Inglis, *School Reports in Westchester County: A Study of Local School Conditions* (White Plains, NY: Westchester County Research Bureau, 1912), 1.
18. Ibid., 22, 23.
19. Ibid., 9–10.
20. Ibid., 22.
21. James Russell to William Demarest, 17 June 1912, William H. S. Demarest Papers, Records Group 4/A11/3, Special Collections and Archives, Rutgers University Libraries.
22. James Russell to William H. Demarest, 17 June 1912, "Notes by E. L. Thorndike," Demarest to Russell, 29 June 1912, Demarest to Thorndike, 29 June 1912, Thorndike to Demarest, 6 July 1912, William H. S. Demarest Papers, Records Group 4/A11/3, Special Collections and Archives, Rutgers University Libraries. For a record of Inglis's arrival at Rutgers College, see *The Targum*, 25 September 1912 and *The Scarlet Letter*, May 1913, Educational Archive, Special Collections and Archives, Rutgers University Libraries.
23. William H. S. Demarest, *A History of Rutgers College, 1766–1924* (New Brunswick, NJ: Rutgers College, 1924), 516; Richard P. McCormick, *Rutgers: A Bicentennial History* (New Brunswick, NJ: Rutgers University Press, 1966), 141ff.
24. Inglis to Demarest, 16 November 1912, with attachments, "Department of Education, 1906–1918," box 12, folder 16, William H. S. Demarest Papers, Records Group 4/A11/3, Special Collections and Archives, Rutgers University Libraries.
25. *Rutgers College Catalog, 1912–13*, 78–9, Special Collections and Archives, Rutgers University Libraries.
26. "Suggested Reorganization of the Courses in Pedagogy," typed manuscript, "Department of Education, 1906–1918," box 12, folder

16, William H. S. Demarest Papers, Records Group 4/A11/3, *Rutgers College Catalog, 1912–13*, 84–5, Special Collections and Archives, Rutgers University Libraries.

27. For example, "Prof. A.J. Inglis Spoke before School Teachers," *Daily Home News*, 11 April 1913, clipping, William H. S. Demarest Papers, Records Group 4/A11/3, Special Collections and Archives, Rutgers University Libraries.
28. "Summer School, 1913–14," box 39, folder 8, William H. S. Demarest Papers, Records Group 4/A11/3, Special Collections and Archives, Rutgers University Libraries.
29. *Rutgers College Department of Education Extension Courses 1913–14*, brochure, "Department of Education, 1906–1918," box 12, folder 16, William H. S. Demarest Papers, Records Group 4/A11/3, Special Collections and Archives, Rutgers University Libraries.
30. Ibid.
31. Alexander Inglis, "The Distribution of Pupils in the Public High School," *Educational Review* (November 1913): 350.
32. Powell, *The Uncertain Profession*, chaps 1–3.
33. Ibid., chaps. 4 and 5.
34. E. L. Thorndike to P. H. Hanus, 23 March 1914, Correspondence of H. W. Holmes, 1913–20, Alexander J. Inglis folder, Harvard University Archives.
35. Inglis to Holmes, 5 September 1914, Inglis to Holmes, 16 September 1914, Correspondence of H. W. Holmes, 1913–20, Alexander J. Inglis folder, Harvard University Archives. For announcements of Inglis's arrival at Harvard, see clippings, "Appointed to Harvard Division of Education," *Boston Herald*, 22 October 1914, "Harvard and Radcliffe Will Train Teachers, *Boston Herald*, 29 January 1915, biographical folder for Alexander J. Inglis, Harvard University Archives.
36. *Official Register, Division of Education, 1915–1916*, 17–22, HUE 22 115.14, Harvard University Archives; "Inglis Material, 1921–22" folder, Correspondence of H. W. Holmes, 1913–20, Harvard University Archives; Inglis, *Principles of Secondary Education*, v.
37. On the conservatism of the community of classicists in the United States at the time, see George A. Kennedy, "Afterword: An Essay on Classics in America Since the Yale Report," in, *Classica Americana: The Greek and Roman Heritage in the United States,* ed. Meyer Reinhold (Detroit, MI: Wayne State University Press, 1984), 340; Ed Phinney, "Introduction," in *The History of the American Classical League, 1919–1994,* ed. Ed Phinney (Oxford, OH: The American Classical League,

1994), 10; Basil L. Gildersleeve, "The Creed of the Old South," *The Atlantic Monthly* 69 (January 1892): 75–87. On the rhetorical nature of defenses of the classics, see Waquet, *Latin or the Empire of a Sign*, and these contemporary arguments of which Inglis may well have been aware: "A Symposium on the Value of the Humanistic, Particularly Classical, Studies as a Preparation for the Study of Law, from the Point of View of the Profession," *School Review* 15 (June 1907): 409–35; "A Symposium on the Value of the Humanistic, Particularly Classical, Studies as a Preparation for the Study of Theology, from the Point of View of the Profession," *School Review* 16 (June 1908): 370–90. "On the Value of the Humanistic, Particularly Classical, Studies as a Training for Men of Affairs," *School Review* 17 (June 1909): 369–403.

38. Gaddis, *Landscape of History*, 120.
39. Ibid., 121, 122.

Chapter Three

1. Contemporary works include William D. Lewis, *Democracy's High School* (Boston: Houghton Mifflin, 1914); Julius Sachs, *The American Secondary School and Some of Its Problems* (NY: Macmillan, 1914); Charles Hughes Johnston, ed., *High School Education* (NY: Charles Scribner's Sons, 1912); Charles Hughes Johnston, ed., *The Modern High School: Its Administration and Extension* (NY: Charles Scribner's Sons, 1914); Paul Monroe, ed., *Principles of Secondary Education* (NY: Macmillan, 1915).
2. *Rutgers College Catalog for 1912–13*, 84, Special Collections and Archives, Rutgers University Libraries; *Official Register, Division of Education, 1915–16*, 17, 19, 22, HUE 22 115.14, Harvard University Archives.
3. Alexander Inglis, "Books and Literature," *School and Society* 1 (2 January 1915): 31.
4. Alexander Inglis, "High-School Graduates and Preparation for Higher Institutions," *School and Society* 1 (26 June 1915): 932–4.
5. Alexander Inglis, "A Fundamental Problem in the Reorganization of the High School," *The School Review* 13 (May 1915): 307–18.
6. Ibid., 318.
7. Alexander Inglis, "The Socialization of the High School," *Teachers College Record* 16 (May 1915): 205–6.
8. Ibid., 206.
9. Ibid.

10. Ibid., 207.
11. Ibid., 209.
12. Ibid., 211.
13. Ibid., 212, 213.
14. Ibid., 216.
15. Alexander J. Inglis, "The Junior High School: Some Principles Affecting Its Organization and Administration," *The Harvard Teachers' Association Leaflet* 2 (October 1916): 1–9; Alexander J. Inglis, "The Junior High School (Outline Presented to the New England Superintendents' Association)," *New England Journal of Education* 84 (14 December 1916): 595–7.
16. Inglis, "The Junior High School: Some Principles," 8.
17. Inglis, "The Junior High School (Outline)," 596.
18. Inglis, "The Junior High School: Some Principles," 8.
19. Franklin S. Hoyt to Inglis, 3 March 1915, folder 5, Inglis to Hoyt, 27 November 1915, folder 1, Correspondence between Alexander James Inglis and Houghton Mifflin, Houghton Library, Harvard University.
20. David Snedden, *Problems of Secondary Education* (Boston: Houghton Mifflin, 1917); Hoyt to Inglis, 3 March 1915, folder 5, Inglis to Cubberly, 16 August 1916, folder 2, Hoyt to Inglis, 19 September 1916, folder 6, Correspondence between Alexander James Inglis and Houghton Mifflin, Houghton Library, Harvard University.
21. Inglis to Hoyt, 16 March 1915, folder 1, Hoyt to Inglis, 19 September 1916, folder 6, Inglis to Foster, 16 August 1916, folder 2, Inglis to Hoyt, 4 December 1916, folder 2, Correspondence between Alexander James Inglis and Houghton Mifflin, Houghton Library, Harvard University.
22. See "Notes," *The Harvard Teachers' Association Leaflet* 2 (October 1916): 10.
23. See Franklin S. Hoyt to Inglis, 17 November 1915, folder 5, and Houghton-Mifflin to Inglis, 31 July 1917, folder 6, and other materials in Correspondence between Alexander James Inglis and Houghton Mifflin, Houghton Library, Harvard University.
24. Inglis, *Principles of Secondary Education*, vi, vii.
25. Ibid., v.
26. Ibid., 46.
27. Ibid., 88.
28. Stanley Coben, "The Assault on Victorianism in the Twentieth Century," in *Victorian America*, ed. Daniel Walker Howe (Philadelphia, PA: University of Pennsylvania Press, 1976), 166, 169.

29. See Nell Irvin Painter, *Standing at Armageddon: The United States, 1877–1919* (NY: Norton, 1987); Michael McGerr, *A Fierce Discontent: The Rise and Fall of the Progressive Movement in America, 1870–1920* (NY: Free Press, 2003), 182ff.
30. Inglis, *Principles of Secondary Education*, 4, 34, 35. For Thorndike on the limitations of educational measurement, see Edward L. Thorndike, "The Nature, Purposes, and General Methods of Measurements of Educational Products," in *The Measurement of Educational Products*, 17th Yearbook of the National Society for the Study of Education, part II (Bloomington, IL: Public School, 1918), 16–24.
31. Inglis, *Principles of Secondary Education*, 295.
32. Ibid., 304.
33. Ibid., 340.
34. Ibid., 341.
35. Ibid., 348.
36. Ibid., 368, 369, 371.
37. Inglis, *Principles of Secondary Education*, 378, 380, 382, 382–83. For a misrepresentation of Inglis's functions of secondary education that appeared unexpectedly in the popular press, see John Taylor Gatto, "Against School: How Public Education Cripples Our Kids, and Why," *Harpers Magazine* 307 (September 2003): 33–38.
38. Inglis, *Principles of Secondary Education*, 387.
39. Ibid., 394.
40. Ibid., 458.
41. Ibid.
42. Ibid., 460. For Lodge's comments, see Andrew West, ed. *Value of the Classics* (Princeton, NJ: Princeton University Press, 1917), 102–3.
43. Inglis, *Principles of Secondary Education*, 567.
44. Ibid., 665–6.
45. Ibid., 674–81.
46. Ibid., 703.
47. Ibid., 711.
48. Ibid., 715.
49. Ibid., 718.
50. Ibid., 720.
51. Miriam F. Carpenter to Houghton Mifflin, 28 January 1918, Inglis to Houghton Mifflin, 4 February 1918, Inglis to Hoyt, 12 February 1918, Inglis to Hoyt, 19 March 1918, folder 4, Correspondence between Alexander James Inglis and Houghton Mifflin, Houghton Library, Harvard University.

52. Hoyt to Inglis, 6 March 1918, folder 7, see also Inglis to Hoyt, 12 March 1918, folder 4, Inglis to Hoyt, 18 March 1918, folder 4, Correspondence between Alexander James Inglis and Houghton Mifflin, bMS Am 1925 (931), Houghton Library, Harvard University. Reproduced by permission of the Houghton Library, Harvard University.
53. "Educational Writings," *The School Review* 26 (March 1918): 226.
54. "Reviews: Education," *The Nation* 106 (4 May 1918): 541.
55. "Record of Book Sales, 1905–1923," MS Am 2030(33), Houghton Mifflin Papers, Houghton Library, Harvard University. Reproduced by permission of the Houghton Library, Harvard University.
56. Snedden, *Problems of Secondary Education.*
57. Richard L. McCormick, "Public Life in Industrial American, 1877–1917," in *The New American History*, ed. Eric Foner (Philadelphia: Temple University Press, 1997), 121, 122.
58. See Robert H. Wiebe, *The Search for Order, 1877–1920* (NY: Hill & Wang, 1967).
59. Gaither, *American Educational History Reconsidered*, 99.
60. Cremin, "The Revolution in American Secondary Education," 295.
61. John L. Childs, *American Pragmatism and Education: An Interpretation and Criticism* (NY: Henry Holt, 1956), 11, 146; see also Louis Menand, *The Metaphysical Club: A Story of Ideas in America* (NY: Farrar, Straus & Giroux, 2001).

Chapter Four

1. See Noah G. Simmons, "The Emerging Design for the Comprehensive American High School, 1913–22" (Doctoral diss., Washington University, 1960); Krug, *The Shaping of the American High School.*
2. Krug, *The Shaping of the American High School*, 387.
3. Works that have recapitulated Krug's interpretation include David B. Tyack, ed., *Turning Points in American Educational History* (Waltham, MA: Blaisdell, 1967); Kliebard, "The Curriculum Field in Retrospect"; T. James and David Tyack, "Learning from Past Efforts to Reform the High School," *Phi Delta Kappan* 64 (1983): 400–6; Kliebard, *The Struggle for the American Curriculum, 1893–1958*; Joel Spring, *The American School, 1642–1990* (NY: Longman, 1990); Herbert M. Kliebard, "The Cardinal Principles Report as Archeological Deposit," *Curriculum Studies* 3 (1995): 197–208; David Tyack and Larry Cuban, *Tinkering Toward Utopia: A Century of Public School Reform* (Cambridge,

MA: Harvard University Press, 1995); Herbst, *The Once and Future School*; Herbert M. Kliebard, *Schooled to Work*; Herbert M. Kliebard, "Cardinal Principles of Secondary Education," in *Historical Dictionary of American Education,* ed. Richard J. Altenbaugh (Westport, CT: Greenwood, 1999), 67–8; Diane Ravitch, *Left Back*; William J. Reese, *America's Public Schools: From the Common School to "No Child Left Behind"* (Baltimore, MD: The Johns Hopkins University Press, 2005). Works that have taken exception to this interpretation include Tanner and Tanner, *History of the School Curriculum* and William G. Wraga, *Democracy's High School: The Comprehensive High School and Educational Reform in the United States* (Lanham, MD: University Press of America, 1994).

4. William G. Wraga, "A Progressive Legacy Squandered: The *Cardinal Principles* Report Reconsidered," *History of Education Quarterly* 41 (Winter 2001): 494–519; also see letters to the editor in *History of Education Quarterly* 42 (Summer 2002), 308–11.
5. Inglis to Holmes, 24 February 1916, Western Union Telegram, Correspondence of H. W. Holmes, 1913–20, Harvard University Archives; "Minutes of Meeting of Reviewing Committee, Detroit, February 20, 21, 22, 1916," "Reorganization of Secondary Education," RG 12, National Archives and Records Administration. See also Clarence D. Kingsley, "Meetings of the Commission on the Reorganization of Secondary Education," *Educational Administration and Supervision* 1 (May 1915): 330–2.
6. Inglis, *Principles of Secondary Education*, 462; Clarence Kingsley to Abraham Flexner, 30 October 1920, Accession No. 23, Series 1, Subseries 2, box 309, folder 3231, General Education Board, 699, Rockefeller Archive Center.
7. "Minutes of Meeting of Reviewing Committee, Detroit, February 20, 21, 22, 1916," Record Group 12, Reorganization of Secondary Education, National Archives and Records Administration; Wraga, "A Progressive Legacy Squandered," 506.
8. "Preliminary Plan for Meeting of the Reviewing Committee," 30 September 1915, Record Group 12, Reorganization of Secondary Education, National Archives and Records Administration.
9. CRSE, *Cardinal Principles of Secondary Education*, 15–16; Wraga, "A Progressive Legacy Squandered," 506.
10. "Draft of Report of Reviewing Committee of the Commission on Secondary Education Appointed by the National Education

Association" (1916), 19, and Kingsley to Members of the Reviewing Committee, 3 June 1916, Record Group 12, Reorganization of Secondary Education, National Archives and Records Administration.

11. CRSE, *Cardinal Principles of Secondary Education*, 21, 23, 24.
12. Alexander Inglis, "The Socialization of the High School."
13. Inglis, "Socialization of the High School," 213.
14. Ibid., 216.
15. CRSE, *Cardinal Principles of Secondary Education*, 21.
16. Ibid., 21, 23.
17. Simmons, "The Emerging Design for the Comprehensive High School, 1913–22," 337–9. See also Daniel Tanner and Laurel Tanner, *Curriculum Development: Theory into Practice* (Englewood Cliffs, NJ: Merrill, 1995), 412.
18. Simmons, "The Emerging Design for the Comprehensive High School, 1913–22," 338.
19. Inglis, *Principles of Secondary Education*, 703.
20. CRSE, *Cardinal Principles of Secondary Education*, 24.
21. Simmons, "The Emerging Design for the Comprehensive High School, 1913–22," 339.
22. Diaries of William Heard Kilpatrick, Entry for 26 February 1917, vol. 13, 36, Accession No. 670403, Special Collections, Milbank Memorial Library, Teachers College, Columbia University.
23. *In Memoriam: Alexander Inglis, 1879–1924* (Cambridge, MA: Harvard University Graduate School of Education, 1925), 8.
24. Ibid., 33.
25. Untitled document in Biographical Folder for Alexander James Inglis, 609, HUG 300, Harvard University Archives.
26. See unpublished memoir of L. Thomas Hopkins, chap. II, 63, L. Thomas Hopkins Collection, box 10, folder 3, Archives, University of Colorado at Boulder Libraries.
27. That Snedden effectively rejected the recommendations of the Commission on the Reorganization of Secondary Education supports this interpretation as well. See David Snedden, "Cardinal Principles of Secondary Education," *School and Society* 9 (3 May 1919): 519, 527.
28. "Announcement by the Editors," *Educational Administration and Supervision* 1 (January 1915): 1.
29. Alexander Inglis, review of *An Introduction to High-School Teaching*, by Stephen Sheldon Colvin, *School and Society* 7 (23 February 1918): 235, 234.

30. Inglis, *Principles of Secondary Education*, 327.
31. Ibid., 329.
32. Alexander Inglis, "Reliability of Grading by the College Entrance Examination Board," *Educational Administration and Supervision* 4 (February 1918): 98.
33. Alexander Inglis, "The Factor of Selection in Grade Distribution," *School and Society* 7 (February 1918): 180.
34. Alexander Inglis, "The War and Secondary Education," *Educational Administration and Supervision* 4 (January 1918): 23–32.
35. Ibid., 24.
36. Ibid., 25, 26.
37. Ibid., 28.
38. Ibid., 30.
39. Memorandum, n.d., RG 165, Records of the War Department and General Staff, War College Division and War Plans Division, Educational and Research Branch, Committee on Education and Special Training, National Archives and Records Administration.
40. *General Orders and Bulletins*, War Department, 1918, RG 165, Records of the War Department and General Staff, National Archives and Records Administration.
41. *Practical Training for Army Service*, 5 April 1918, pamphlet, RG 165, Records of the War Department and General Staff, War College Division and War Plans Division, Educational and Research Branch, Committee on Education and Special Training, box 02, entry 415, National Archives and Records Administration.
42. Richard C. Maclauvin to Lowell, 18 October 1918, Lowell Papers, file 441, Harvard University Archives.
43. A 1937 brochure for the Al Inglis Scholarship Award of Wesleyan University listed his title at CEST as assistant to the director, Collegiate Section, Student Army Training Corps, collection of author. No documentation, however, of Inglis's activities were located in the CEST files at the National Archives and Records Administration. A certificate of his service to the CEST, though, signed by Newton Baker, was among the effects that David Brooks, Inglis's nephew, provided the author.
44. *Virginia Public Schools Education Commission's Report to the Assembly of Virginia* (Richmond, VA: Everett Waddey, 1919), 12; Inglis to Holmes, 19 December 1918, Correspondence of H. W. Holmes, UAV 350.20, box He-Na, Alexander Inglis File, Harvard University Archives.

Chapter Five

1. Hollis L. Caswell, *City School Surveys: An Interpretation and Appraisal*, Teachers College Contributions to Education No. 358 (NY: Teachers College Bureau of Publications, 1929).
2. Edgar W. Knight, *Education in the United States*, 2nd ed. (Boston: Ginn, 1941), 548.
3. Newton Edwards and Herman C. Richey, *The School in the American Social Order* (Boston: Houghton Mifflin, 1947), 800. See also Newton Edwards and Herman C. Richey, *The School in the American Social Order*, 2nd ed. (Boston: Houghton Mifflin, 1963), 612–13; John S. Brubacher, *A History of the Problems of Education* (NY: McGraw-Hill, 1947), 558–9; Isaac L. Kandel, *American Education in the Twentieth Century* (Cambridge, MA: Harvard University Press, 1957), 36, 38.
4. Raymond E. Callahan, *Education and the Cult of Efficiency* (Chicago: University of Chicago Press, 1962), 112.
5. Ibid., 116–17.
6. Krug, *The Shaping of the American High School*, 323.
7. Tyack, *The One Best System*, 191.
8. Ibid., 196. See also Tyack and Hansot, *Managers of Virtue*; Kliebard, *The Struggle for the American Curriculum, 1893–1958*, 187; Kliebard, *Schooled to Work*, 153, also 154–5; Ravitch, *Left Back*, 107.
9. Ellen Condliffe Lagemann, *An Elusive Science: The Troubling History of Educational Research* (Chicago: University of Chicago Press, 2000), 80, 81, 87, also 233.
10. A. Inglis to A. Flexner, 24 October 1919, A. Flexner to A. Inglis, 31 October 1919, A. Inglis to A. Flexner, 3 November 1919, A. Flexner to A. Inglis, 6 November 1919, A Inglis to A. Flexner, 10 November 1919, General Education Board Series 1, Subseries 2, box 188, folder 1767, Virginia Survey 1918–23, Rockefeller Archive Center; *In Memorium: Alexander Inglis, 1879–1924*, 43, 48.
11. George D. Strayer, *Report of the Survey of the Public School System of Baltimore, Maryland*, 3 vols (Baltimore: Board of School Commissioners, 1921). "The Report of the Reviewing Committee" appears in vol. 2, viii–x, and also in vol. 3. For a depiction of the Baltimore survey as manifesting social efficiency–social control doctrine, see Kliebard, *Schooled to Work*, 153–7.
12. Callahan, *Education and the Cult of Efficiency*, 116, 244ff.
13. Inglis, *School Reports in Westchester County*, 1.
14. Ibid., 22.

15. *A Survey of Educational Institutions in the State of Washington*, Bulletin 1916, No. 26, Department of the Interior, Bureau of Education (Washington, DC: U.S. Government Printing Office, 1916).
16. *The Educational System of South Dakota*, Bulletin 1918, No. 31, Department of the Interior, Bureau of Education (Washington, DC: U.S. Government Printing Office, 1918), 272.
17. Ibid., 282.
18. Ibid., 283.
19. Ibid., 286–7.
20. *Virginia Public Schools Education Commission's Report*, plates facing 70, 204, 206.
21. *A Survey of the Schools of Swansea, Massachusetts, June 1920*, in *Annual Reports of the Town Offices of the Town of Swansea* (for the year ending December 31, 1920) (Fall River, MA: B.R. Acornley, 1921), 23.
22. Ibid., 24.
23. *Report of Survey Staff to Board of Education* (Augusta, MN: Kennebec Journal Print Shop, 1922), 19–20.
24. Ibid., 196.
25. Ibid., 197.
26. Callahan, *Education and the Cult of Efficiency*, 244. The report of the six-member reviewing committee of the Baltimore survey recommended no cost-cutting measures, as well. It neither used the term *efficiency* nor appealed to business values. In fact, the Baltimore survey resulted in a $ 22 million dollar building campaign, among other expenditures. See Strayer, *Report of the Survey of the Public School System of Baltimore, Maryland*, vol. 2, viii–x; George D. Strayer, "A Comprehensive School Survey and Its Consequences," *Addresses and Proceedings of the Sixty-First Annual Meeting* (Washington, DC: National Education Association, 1923), 1016–1018.
27. Tyack, *The One Best System*, 126–129, 196.
28. *Virginia Public Schools Education Commission's Report*, 269, 262.
29. *Report of Survey Staff to [Augusta] Board of Education*, 174.
30. *Virginia Public Schools Education Commission's Report*, chaps III, II, VII, XXI, and XV.
31. Strayer, *Report of the Survey of the Public School System of Baltimore, Maryland*, vol. 2, viii.
32. *A Survey of the Schools of Swansea*, 24–9.
33. *Virginia Public Schools Education Commission's Report*, 216, 215, 210.

34. Indiana Education Survey Commission, *Public Education in Indiana* (NY: General Education Board, 1923), 113–14.
35. *Report of Survey Staff to [Augusta] Board of Education*, 176.
36. Strayer, *Report of the Survey of the Public School System of Baltimore, Maryland*, vol. 2, viii. This administrative team would include at least one woman; see Strayer, "A Comprehensive School Survey and Its Consequences," 1017.
37. *Virginia Public Schools Education Commission's Report*, 229–30.
38. *A Survey of the Schools of Swansea*, 24–29.
39. Strayer, *Report of the Survey of the Public School System of Baltimore, Maryland*, vol. 2, ix–x.
40. Indiana Education Survey Commission, *Public Education in Indiana*, 107–8.
41. Ibid., 108.
42. Ibid.
43. Tyack, *The One Best System*, 197.
44. Ibid.
45. CRSE, *Cardinal Principles of Secondary Education*.
46. Krug, *The Shaping of the American High School*, 323, 325; Kliebard, *The Struggle for the American Curriculum, 1893–1958*, 187; Kliebard, *Schooled to Work*, 153.
47. *Virginia Public Schools Education Commission's Report*, 177.
48. Ibid.
49. Ibid.
50. Ibid., 132.
51. "Psychological and Educational Tests in the Public Schools of Winchester, Virginia," report printed in *University of Virginia Record* 6 (January 1922): 11.
52. Ibid., 7.
53. Inglis and Dearborn found, however, that in general teachers' judgments were unreliable, usually undermined by self-fulfilling expectations.
54. "Psychological and Educational Tests in the Public Schools of Winchester, Virginia," 24.
55. See Paul D. Chapman, *Schools as Sorters: Louis M. Terman, Applied Psychology, and the Intelligence Testing Movement, 1890–1930* (NY: New York University Press, 1988).
56. "Psychological and Educational Tests in the Public Schools of Winchester," 26–7.
57. Ibid., 27.

58. See Chapman, *Schools as Sorters*, 153.
59. *A Survey of the Schools of Swansea*, 5.
60. Ibid.
61. Ibid., 7.
62. Ibid., 21.
63. Ibid., 22.
64. Ibid., 26.
65. *Report of Survey Staff to [Augusta] Board of Education*, 50.
66. Ibid., 51.
67. Ibid., 9.
68. Ibid., 90.
69. Ibid., 93. The reviewing committee of the Baltimore survey recommended the junior high school as well; see Strayer, *Report of the Survey of the Public School System of Baltimore, Maryland*, vol. 2, ix.
70. See Inglis, "The Socialization of the High School"; Inglis, "A Fundamental problem in the Reorganization of the High School"; Inglis, "The Junior High School: Some Principles Affecting Its Organization and Administration"; Inglis, *Principles of Secondary Education*.
71. Indiana Education Survey Commission, *Public Education in Indiana*, 33.
72. Ibid., 28–9.
73. Ibid., 32.
74. Angus and Mirel, *The Failed Promise of the American High School*; Ravitch, *Left Back*. These interpretations echo criticisms of progressive education leveled during the 1950s by popular school critics. See, for example, Arthur E. Bestor, Jr, *Educational Wastelands: The Retreat from Learning in Our Public Schools* (Urbana, IL: University of Illinois Press, 1953); John F. Latimer, *What's Happened to Our High Schools?* (Washington, DC: Public Affairs Press, 1958).
75. Indiana Education Survey Commission, *Public Education in Indiana*, 126, 127.
76. Ibid., 127.
77. Ibid., 127–8.
78. *Virginia Public Schools Education Commission's Report*, 220.
79. Ibid., 201.
80. McGerr, *A Fierce Discontent*, 215.
81. *Virginia Public Schools Education Commission's Report*, 171.
82. Ibid., 131.
83. Ibid.

84. Ibid., plates facing 70, 204, 206.
85. Ibid., 41.
86. Ibid., 198.
87. Ibid., 201.
88. Ibid., 41.
89. McGerr, *A Fierce Discontent*, 188.
90. See James D. Anderson, *The Education of Blacks in the South, 1860–1935* (Chapel Hill: University of North Carolina Press, 1988), 199, 202–3; Eric Anderson and Alfred A. Moss, Jr, *Dangerous Donations: Northern Philanthropy and Southern Black Education* (Columbia: University of Missouri Press, 1999), 95–100; Michael E. James, *The Conspiracy of the Good: Civil Rights and the Struggle for Community in Two American Cities, 1875–2000* (NY: Peter Lang, 2005), 100–3.
91. CRSE, *Cardinal Principles of Secondary Education*, 19, 23, 25, 21.
92. Callahan, *Education and the Cult of Efficiency*, 116–17; Tyack, *The One Best System*, 197; Lagemann, *An Elusive Science*, 80, 81.

Chapter Six

1. Course catalogs at Harvard listed Inglis as the instructor for all of the secondary education courses from his appointment in 1914 until the early 1920s. During this period the number of secondary education courses increased from four to nine. See, for example, *Official Register*, Division of Education, 1915–16, 17, 19, 22, HUE 22 115.14, Harvard University Archives. After the Division of Education became the Graduate School of Education in 1920, the course catalog was called, simply, *Graduate School of Education*; see the catalogs for academic years 1921 through 1924 at Special Collections, Monroe C. Gutman Library, Graduate School of Education, Harvard University. Also see *Official Register, Division of Education, 1915–1916*, 17–22, HUE 22 115.14, Harvard University Archives; "Inglis Material, 1921–22" folder, Correspondence of H. W. Holmes, 1913–20, Harvard University Archives. Cf. Geraldine Jonich Clifford and James W. Guthrie, *Ed School: A Brief for Professional Education* (Chicago: University of Chicago Press, 1988), 102.
2. *Graduate School of Education, 1920–21*, 44, Special Collections, Monroe C. Gutman Library, Graduate School of Education, Harvard University.
3. Ibid., 48, 49.
4. *In Memorium: Alexander Inglis, 1879–1924*, 15, 16, 18.

5. Unpublished memoir of L. Thomas Hopkins, chap. II, 62, L. Thomas Hopkins Collection, box 10, folder 3, Archives, University of Colorado at Boulder Libraries.
6. Ibid., 64, 62.
7. Holmes to Inglis, 15 March 1919, Papers of W. H. Holmes, Correspondence 1913–20, UAV.350.20, box He-Ha, Division of Education, Harvard University Archives.
8. Inglis to Holmes, 20 March 1919, Papers of W. H. Holmes, Correspondence 1913–20, UAV.350.20, box He-Ha, Division of Education, Harvard University Archives.
9. Powell, *The Uncertain Profession*, 134–6; see also Paul H. Hanus, *Adventuring in Education* (Cambridge, MA: Harvard University Press, 1937).
10. Holmes to Lowell, 15 March 1919, Lowell Papers, Harvard University Archives. The survey Holmes reported was George S. Counts, "The General Course in Secondary Education in American Colleges and Universities," *Educational Monographs* (The Society of College Teachers of Education), no. 8 (1919): 41.
11. Holmes to Inglis, 15 March 1919, Papers of W. H. Holmes, Correspondence 1913–20, UAV.350.20, box He-Ha, Division of Education, Harvard University Archives.
12. Inglis to Holmes, 20 March 1919, Papers of W. H. Holmes, Correspondence 1913–20, UAV.350.20, box He-Ha, Division of Education, Harvard University Archives.
13. Holmes to Inglis, 8 April 1919, Papers of W. H. Holmes, Correspondence 1913–20, UAV.350.20, box He-Ha, Division of Education, Harvard University Archives.
14. Holmes to Inglis, 30 March 1920, telegram, Correspondence and Papers of the Dean, W. H. Holmes, UAV.350.20, 1919/1920, box I-S, Graduate School of Education, Harvard University Archives.
15. "Brief for the Admission of Women as Students and Candidates for Degrees in the Graduate School of Education," 30 March 1920, "Inglis Material, 1921–22" file, Correspondence and Papers of the Dean, W. H. Holmes, UAV.350.30, box 1, Graduate School of Education, Harvard University Archives. Cf. Clifford and Guthrie, *Ed School*, 100; see Powell, *The Uncertain Profession*, 139.
16. "Inglis Material, 1921–22" file, Correspondence and Papers of the Dean, W. H. Holmes, UAV.350.30, box 1, Graduate School of Education, Harvard University Archives.

17. "Inglis, Alexander James," *National Cyclopedia of American Biography*, vol. 23 (NY: James T. White, 1933), 54. Personal communication from Linda McDaniels, American Association for the Advancement of Science, 11 January 2001.
18. *A History of the National Society of College Teachers of Education, 1902–1950* (The Society, 1950), 4.
19. Ibid. The Society of College Teachers of Education, *Studies in Education*, Educational Monographs Number 11 (Baltimore, MD: J. H. Furst, 1922). The NSCTE continues today; in 1969 it was renamed the Society of Professors of Education.
20. Tyack and Hansot, *Managers of Virtue*, 131–3.
21. "The Cleveland Conference, 1915–1925" with attachment "Outline of Major Issues Discussed by the Cleveland Conference," "The Cleveland Conference, 1915-1949," Charles Judd to Members of the Cleveland Conference, 14 January 1918, "Present Members of the Cleveland Conference," n.d., "Members of the Cleveland Conference—1920," "Members of the Cleveland Conference—1921," "Cleveland Conference—1923," Charles Chadsey to Members of the Cleveland Conference, 16 November 1923, folders 1, 2, and 4, box 1, Cleveland Conference Records, Special Collections Research Center, University of Chicago Library.
22. Edgar B. Wesley, *NEA: The First Hundred Years* (NY: Harper, 1957), 243ff.
23. For advocacy of the bill, see Horace Mann Towner, "National Aid for Education," *NEA Addresses and Proceedings*, 59th Annual Meeting (Washington, DC: NEA, 1921), 786–95; "Committee Reports Education Bill," *The Journal of the National Education Association* 10 (March 1921): 41; Hugh S. Magill, "Education and the Federal Government," *The Journal of the National Education Association* 10 (November 1921): 155–8; "The Towner-Sterling Bill," *The Journal of the National Education Association* 11 (April 1922): 150; George D. Strayer, "The Towner-Sterling Bill," *The Journal of the National Education Association* 11 (October 1922): 311–14.
24. Alexander Inglis, "Federal Policies in Education," *Educational Record* 3 (April 1922): 119, 120. Inglis presented this paper to the NEA's Department of Superintendence as part of a panel at the Association's annual meeting on 22 February 1922. See Alexander Inglis, "The Need of a National Organization for Educational Service," *Addresses and Proceedings of the Sixtieth Annual Meeting*, vol. 60 (Washington, DC: NEA, 1922), 1322–30.

25. Inglis, "Federal Policies in Education," 121.
26. Ibid., 122.
27. Ibid., 123–4.
28. See P. H. DuBois, *A History of Psychological Testing* (Boston: Allyn & Bacon, 1970); Chapman, *Schools as Sorters.*
29. Alexander Inglis, *Intelligence Quotient Values* (Yonkers-on-Hudson, NY: World Book, 1921); Alexander Inglis, "A Vocabulary Test for High-School and College Students," *The English Leaflet* 23 (October 1923): 1–13.
30. *Reports of the President and Treasurer of Harvard College, 1922–1923,* "The Graduate School of Education," 162, Harvard University Archives. The Inglis Latin tests, along with one manual and three correction keys, are in the Historical Textbook Collection, Monroe C. Gutman Library, Graduate School of Education, Harvard University. These tests were published in 1927, after Inglis's death.
31. "Report of the Dean of the Graduate School of Education, Harvard University," contained in the *Report of the President of Harvard University, 1922–23,* 161–2, Special Collections, Monroe C. Gutman Library, Graduate School of Education, Harvard University.
32. Alexander Inglis, "A Vocabulary Test for High-School and College Students."
33. Ibid., 9; emphasis in original.
34. Ibid., 13.
35. Chapman, *Schools as Sorters,* 153ff.
36. On Inglis's recommendations for using tests to a school system he surveyed, see "Psychological and Educational Tests in the Public Schools of Winchester, Virginia," 26, 27. On flexibility in curriculum differentiations, see Inglis, *Principles of Secondary Education,* 679.
37. See John Dewey, "Mediocrity and Individuality," in *The Middle Works of John Dewey, 1899–1924,* vol. 13, ed. J. A. Boydston (Carbondale: Southern Illinois University Press, 1988), 289–94, originally published in 1922 in *The New Republic.*
38. A. Inglis to A. West, 1 June 1922, Graduate School, Andrew West Series, box 17, folder 4, Mudd Manuscript Library, Princeton University.
39. Inglis, *Principles of Secondary Education,* 458.
40. West, *Value of the Classics.*
41. A. Inglis to A. Flexner, 19 September 1922, Accession No. 23, Series 1, Subseries 2, box 309, folder 3232, General Education Board, 699, Rockefeller Archive Center.

42. Abraham Flexner, "A Modern School," *The American Review of Reviews* 53 (April 1916): 465–74; Winterer, *Culture of Classicism*; Waquet, *Latin or the Empire of a Sign*; Carl A. Jessen and Lester B. Herlihy, *Offerings and Registrations in High School Subjects, 1933–34*, Bulletin 1938, No. 6, Office of Education, Department of the Interior (Washington, DC: U.S. Government Printing Office, 1938), 28; National Center for Educational Statistics, *Digest of Educational Statistics 2002*, 69, 127.
43. Alexander Inglis, "The Conditions of Success in Teaching the Classics," *The Classical Journal* 18 (1922): 10.
44. Ibid., 11.
45. Ibid.
46. Ibid., 12.
47. Ibid., 12–13.
48. Ibid., 13.
49. Ibid., 13–14.
50. Ibid., 14.
51. Ibid., 15.
52. Ibid.
53. Ibid.
54. Ibid., 18.
55. Ibid., 17.
56. Alexander Inglis, "Classical and Native Elements in the English Language," *The Classical Journal* 20 (June 1925): 515–25.
57. Ralph W. Walter, "Prof. Inglis's Language Project," 27 June 1924, Bancroft Beatley to H. W. Holmes, 1 August 1924, Correspondence of H. W. Holmes, Harvard University Archives.
58. Alexander J. Inglis, "Co-operation and Correlation in Language Teaching in the High School."
59. Inglis, "Classical and Native Elements."
60. Ibid., 522, 524.
61. Ibid., 524–5.
62. See Inglis, *Principles of Secondary Education*, 447–80; Inglis, "The Conditions of Success in Teaching the Classics."
63. Bancroft Beatley to H. W. Holmes, 1 August 1924, Correspondence of H. W. Holmes, Harvard University Archives.
64. Inglis, "Classical and Native Elements," 520. That is, *the, of, and, to, a, in, that, it, is,* and *I*—all of Anglo-Saxon origin.
65. Ibid., 515–16. B. L. Ullman, "Our Latin-English Language," *The Classical Journal* 18 (November 1922): 83.

66. Inglis, "Classical and Native Elements," 517; Ullman, "Our Latin-English Language," 83.
67. Inglis, "Classical and Native Elements," 518; Ullman, "Our Latin-English Language," 86.
68. Inglis, "Classical and Native Elements," 524–5; Ullman, "Our Latin-English Language," 83, also 90.
69. Advisory Committee of the American Classical League, *The Classical Investigation: Part One, General Report* (Princeton, NJ: Princeton University Press, 1924), 9, 10.
70. Ibid., 182, 151.
71. Ibid., 187, 229.
72. Ibid., 45.
73. Ibid., 209–10.
74. Ibid., 257, 258.
75. Ibid., 32, 78, 167, 189–91, 202–3.
76. Alexander Inglis, "The High School in Evolution," *The New Republic* (7 November 1923), 1.
77. Ibid., 2.
78. See, for example, Ravitch, *Left Back*; Angus and Mirel, *The Failed Promise of the American High School.*
79. Inglis, "The High School in Evolution," 2, emphasis in original.
80. Ibid., 2.
81. Ibid., 3.
82. Alexander Inglis, "Secondary Education," in *Twenty-Five Years of American Education: Collected Essays*, ed. I. L. Kandel (NY: Macmillan, 1924), 251–69.
83. Ibid., 254, 253.
84. Ibid., 257–8.
85. Ibid., 260–1.
86. Ibid, 265.
87. Ibid.
88. Ibid., 267.
89. Ibid.
90. Ibid., 268; see Inglis, *Principles of Secondary Education*, 381–2.

Chapter Seven

1. H. W. Holmes to Charles K. Bliss, 17 June 1924, Secretary of H. W. Holmes to Dr Bird T. Baldwin, 14 May 1924, Alexander Inglis

File, Correspondence of H. W. Holmes, UAV 350.20, box He-Na, Harvard University Archives; "Alexander J. Inglis," *Middletown Press*, 14 April 1924, Russell Library, Middletown, CT. Obituaries include *Boston Evening News*, 12 April 1924; *New York Times*, 13 April 1924, 27; *School and Society* 19 (3 May 1924): 516–17; *Educational Administration and Supervision* 10 (May 1924): 265–6; *The School Review* 23 (June 1924): 401–2; *The Wesleyan University Alumnus* 8 (May 1924): 23, 38.

2. "Report of the Dean, Graduate School of Education," contained in the *Report of the President of Harvard University, 1923–24*, 157–8, Special Collections, Monroe C. Gutman Library, Graduate School of Education, Harvard University.
3. "Report of the Dean, Graduate School of Education," contained in the *Report of the President of Harvard University, 1923–24*, 158, Special Collections, Monroe C. Gutman Library, Graduate School of Education, Harvard University; Powell, *The Uncertain Profession*, 152.
4. W. Kilpatrick to H. W. Holmes, 27 May 1924, Correspondence and papers of H. W. Holmes, box 1, UAV. 350.30, Harvard University Archives.
5. *In Memorium: Alexander Inglis, 1879–1924*, 27, 56.
6. Ibid., 3, 66, 67, 8.
7. "Inglis Memorial Lectures" folder, "Inglis Tests" folder, H. Holmes to A. C. Inglis, 19 November 1924, Correspondence and Papers of Dean Holmes, 1924–5, box H-NEA, UAV 350.30, Harvard University Archives.
8. Introductory Comments Inglis Lectureship [handwritten], 13 January 1925, Correspondence and Papers of Dean Holmes, 1925–6, box F-L, UAV 350.30, Harvard University Archives; "Wesleyan Sets Up Al Inglis Memorial," *The Middletown Press*, 9 September 1937, 1, Russell Library, Middletown, CT; "Al Inglis Scholarship Award of Wesleyan University," pamphlet, collection of author.
9. A. C. Inglis to H. Holmes, n.d., "Inglis Lecture, 1937–38" folder, Correspondence and Papers of Dean Holmes, 1937–8, box Coo-M, A. C. Inglis to H. Holmes, 16 April 1939, Correspondence and Papers of Dean Holmes, 1938–39, box E-L, UAV 350.30, Harvard University Archives; *Who's Who of American Women*, 632; President and Fellows of Harvard College to Mrs Alexander J. Inglis, 15 December 1955, Nathan M. Pusey to Mrs Alexander J. Inglis, 21 February 1956, collection of author; Meredith W. Canavan, letter to author, 13 June 1996.
10. Krug, *The Shaping of the American High School*, 465; Sizer, *Secondary Schools at the Turn of the Century*, 288–9; Michael B. Katz, *The Irony of*

Early School Reform (Cambridge, MA: Harvard University Press, 1968), 283; Reese, *The Origins of the American High School*, 271.

11. Simmons, "The Emerging Design for the Comprehensive American High School," 337; see, for example, Edgar M. Draper and Alexander C. Roberts, *Principles of American Secondary Education* (NY: D. Appleton-Century, 1932), 207, 223; Thomas H. Briggs, *Secondary Education* (NY: Macmillan, 1935), 67, 80, 102, 297; Rudyard K. Bent and Henry H. Kronenberg, *Principles of Secondary Education* (NY: McGraw-Hill, 1941), 57, 60, 66, 238; J. Paul Leonard, *Developing the Secondary School Curriculum* (NY: Rinehart, 1946), 20; Thomas H. Briggs, J. Paul Leonard, and Joseph Justman, *Secondary Education* (NY: Macmillan, 1950), 54, 176, 204; Will French, *Behavioral Goals of General Education in High School* (NY: Russell Sage Foundation, 1957), 21; Edward A. Krug, *The Secondary School Curriculum* (NY: Harper, 1960), 15, 31, 496; L. O. Taylor, Don R. McMahill, and Bob L. Taylor, *The American Secondary School* (NY: Appleton-Century-Crofts, 1960), 36; Harold Alberty and Elsie J. Alberty, *Reorganizing the High School Curriculum* (NY: Macmillan, 1962), 204.
12. Carl G. F. Franzen, *Foundations of Secondary Education* (NY: Harper & Brothers, 1955), 4.
13. See James B. Conant, *My Several Lives* (NY: Harper & Row, 1970), 613ff; James Bryant Conant, *The Child, the Parent, and the State* (Cambridge, MA: Harvard University Press, 1959).
14. James B. Conant, *The American High School Today* (NY: McGraw-Hill, 1959).
15. Conant, *The Child, the Parent, and the State*, 197–202, 92, 93, 103; James Bryant Conant, *The Revolutionary Transformation of the American High School* (Cambridge, MA: Harvard University Press, 1959).
16. Henry W. Holmes, "Minute on the Life and Services of Professor Alexander James Inglis," 3, forwarded to William G. Inglis by Bancroft Beatley, 29 October 1924, collection of the author. Cf. Powell, *The Uncertain Profession*, 112–13, and Clifford and Guthrie, *Ed School*, 102.
17. L. Thomas Hopkins, *Curriculum Principles and Practices* (NY: Benjamin H. Sanborn, 1929), iii.
18. Daniel Walker Howe, "Victorian Culture in America," in *Victorian America*, ed. Daniel Walker Howe (Philadelphia: University of Pennsylvania Press, 1976), 17.
19. Richard L. McCormick, "Public Life in Industrial American, 1877–1917," in *The New American History*, ed. Eric Foner (Philadelphia: Temple University Press, 1997), 121, 122; Arthur S. Link and Richard

L. McCormick, *Progressivism* (Arlington Heights, IL: Harlan Davidson, 1983), 85.

20. See Wiebe, *The Search for Order, 1877–1920.*
21. See Chapman, *Schools as Sorters*, 5.
22. William L. O'Neill, *The Progressive Years: America Comes of Age* (NY: Harper & Row, 1975), 97, 157.
23. Daniel T. Rodgers, "In Search of Progressivism," *Reviews in American History* 10 (December 1982): 123; McGerr, *A Fierce Discontent*, 215.
24. Link and McCormick, *Progressivism*, 21.
25. See, for example, Link and McCormick, *Progressivism*, 23; Tyack and Hansot, *Managers of Virtue*, 115.
26. McCormick, "Public Life in Industrial America," 124–5, 121.
27. Ibid., 129; Inglis, "The Junior High School: Some Principles Affecting Its Organization and Administration," 8; Inglis, "Federal Policies in Education."
28. Nicholas Lemann, *The Big Test: The Secret History of the American Meritocracy* (NY: Farrar, Straus, & Giroux), 1999; David F. Labaree, *How to Succeed in School Without Really Learning: The Credentials Race in American Education* (New Haven, CT: Yale University Press, 1997).
29. Lagemann, *An Elusive Science*, 73–5.
30. Gaither, *American Educational History Revisited*, 99.
31. Childs, *American Pragmatism and Education*, 11, 142ff.
32. Krug, *The Shaping of the American High School*; Callahan, *Education and the Cult of Efficiency*; Tyack, *The One Best System*; Kliebard, *The Struggle for the American Curriculum, 1893–1958.*
33. *School Reports in Westchester County*, 22; *The Educational System of South Dakota*, 282; *Public Education in Indiana*, 32; *Report of Survey Staff to [Augusta] Board of Education*, 196.
34. Wraga, *Democracy's High School.*
35. Historians of the progressive era have identified at least four meanings of the term as it was used during the early twentieth century; see O'Neill, *The Progressive Years*, 97. Educational and curriculum historians have recognized only a restrictive meaning of the term; for a recent analysis of this problem, see J. Wesley Null, "Social Efficiency Splintered: Multiple Meanings Instead of the Hegemony of One," *Journal of Curriculum and Supervision* 19 (Winter 2004): 99–124.
36. Inglis, *School Reports in Westchester County*, 22.
37. Rodgers, "In Search of Progressivism," 120.
38. Inglis, *Principles of Secondary Education*, 4, 34, 35, 327.
39. *In Memoriam: Alexander Inglis*, 24–25.

40. Gaddis, *The Landscape of History*, 122.
41. Alan Brinkley, "Prosperity, Depression, and War," in *The New American History*, ed. Eric Foner (Philadelphia: Temple University Press, 1997), 138.
42. Unpublished memoirs, chap. II, 62, L. Thomas Hopkins Collection, box 10, folder 3, Archives, University of Colorado at Boulder Libraries.
43. Lawrence A. Cremin, *The Transformation of the School: Progressivism in American Education, 1876–1957* (NY: Knopf, 1962), viii–ix; Inglis, *Principles of Secondary Education*, 612, 39, 70, 626; Inglis, "Secondary Education."
44. *Virginia Public Schools Education Commission's Report*, 246, 262, 269; *Report of Survey Staff to [Augusta] Board of Education*, 174.
45. Indiana Education Survey Commission, *Public Education in Indiana*, 113–14; *Virginia Public Schools Education Commission's Report*, 216, 215, 210.
46. Inglis, "The High School in Evolution," 2; Inglis, "Secondary Education."
47. Tyack, *The One Best System*, 197.
48. Angus and Mirel, *The Failed Promise of the American High School*, 198; Diane Ravitch, *Left Back*, 16, 459. Cf. Kliebard, *The Struggle for the American Curriculum, 1893–1958*. Nor is the anti subject matter extremism of the child-centered progressives evident. See William J. Reese, "The Origins of Progressive Education," *History of Education Quarterly* 41 (Spring 2001): 1–24.
49. Inglis, "The Conditions of Success in Teaching the Classics"; Inglis, "The High School in Evolution"; Indiana Education Survey Committee, *Public Education in Indiana*, 28–9. For his critique of academic formalism in the teaching of, for example, English, mathematics, and the social sciences, see Inglis, *Principles of Secondary Education*, 443, 502–3, and 567, respectively.
50. Kliebard, "The Curriculum Field in Retrospect," 69–84; Powell, *Uncertain Profession*, 112–14; Tanner and Tanner, *History of the School Curriculum*, 363–4.
51. Marc Depaepe, "Demythologizing the Educational Past: An Endless Task in History of Education," *Historical Studies in Education/Revue D'Histoire de L'Education* 9 (1997): 221.
52. Peter Cunningham, "Innovators, Networks, and Structures: Towards a Prosopography of Progressivism," *History of Education* 30 (2001): 433–51. Members of the Cleveland Conference, for example, would be suitable subjects for such a study.

53. Larry Cuban, *How Teachers Taught: Constancy and Change in American Classrooms, 1880–1990* (NY: Teachers College Press, 1993).
54. Van Wyck Brooks, "On Creating a Usable Past," *The Dial* 64 (1918): 337–41.
55. Inglis, *Principles of Secondary Education*, 348.
56. Ibid., 377, 378. See also Will French, *Behavioral Goals of General Education in High School*, 21.

Index